HEART CONDITIONS

HEART CONDITIONS

▼

Vanda Millien

Writers Club Press
San Jose New York Lincoln Shanghai

Heart Conditions

Writers Club Press
an imprint of iUniverse.com, Inc.

For information address:
iUniverse.com, Inc.
620 North 48th Street, Suite 201
Lincoln, NE 68504-3467
www.iuniverse.com

ISBN: 0-595-14086-6

Printed in the United States of America

CONTENTS

THE READER WILL BETTER UNDERSTAND
CERTAIN ASPECTS OF THE TEACHINGS
IN THIS BOOK IF IT IS NOTED THAT THEY
WERE PRESENTED ORALLY.

ACKNOWLEDGMENTS

I would like to express my grateful thanks for all those who contributed to this book, some without even realizing their contribution:

Jean, for her painstaking efforts as a writer and editor which played such a major role in the production of the book.

Everyone who has ever attended my workshops. Thank you for your love and support.

My husband David, for truly being "the wind beneath my wings."

My precious daughters, Nikki and Vanessa for giving me the gift of Motherhood.

My sister Julie, whose winning battle over cancer has helped me to re-define the word courage!

My grandsons, Jacee and Zackary, for re-introducing me to the wonder of life.

My son-in-law, Mike…the son I never had.

My dear friend Regan, just for being "Regan"!

Last, but not least, to God who has given me the sunshine as well as the manure, in the garden of life, enabling me to grow into a strong and colorful flower. Gently, and sometimes not so tenderly, pruning me and whispering by the wind of His Spirit: "Don't give up yet, it's just another 'Heart Condition'"!

PREFACE

For many years I have received requests at my seminars and workshops for a book containing the teachings I have been so privileged to deliver over the last fifteen years.

As I do with all situations, I asked for a sign from the Spirit that this proposed book was in accordance with Divine Will and would manifest at the appropriate time. One week later, at the end of a meeting, a lady who is also an author, suggested the teachings be put in book form! Hence *Heart Conditions* was born.

Everyone has a heart condition, whether spiritual, physical, or both. This book will help you to recognize your heart condition and, consequently, to change it by shifting your spiritual and physical chemistry through forgiveness, compassion and love.

The teachings are by simple stories, taken from the experiences and heartbreaks in my life, suggesting how we can collectively transmute our life experiences into personal mastery.

It is time for us all to leave behind the repressive conditioning and opinions of society and change our own heart conditions by allowing, forgiving, and loving.

This collection of stories will help you to be courageous enough to take responsibility for who you are and to live your own truth.

REJECTION GIVES DIRECTION

PART ONE

▼

REJECTION OF THE HEART

Turning Rejection into Direction

In every seemingly negative situation, there is also a positive side. What is the positive part of rejection? In my personal life, I feel that rejection has given me new direction. Always. When a door has closed—and many, many have—then I find direction through that rejection. I've kicked a few doors down, mind you, and I've had a few splinters and flat noses to prove it. Basically speaking, however, rejection is a positive and directive force.

When I lived in England, I felt that the country rejected me. My parents rejected me, the class system in England rejected me. My grandma was the only one who gave me love when I was growing up. One time I asked her, "Grandma, why do my parents not love me?"

She said, "When you were born, your father wanted a boy. When a girl arrived, he, in effect, sarcastically said, "Drown it." I'm sure that when I was a tiny child I must have felt these vibrations very strongly.

My grandma told me that when my mother asked my father what she should call me, my father said, "Call it Wanda."

Since my father was Polish, my mother knew that he got his "V's" and "W's" mixed up, so she named me Vanda.

Four or five years ago I went to a retreat in California. We were studying Eastern philosophy and were to observe four days of silence. When I arrived and went in to register, I was feeling a little low. The lady at the desk asked me my name, and I said, "It's Vanda." And she asked, "Is that your real name?" I said, "Yes, of course."

"Do you know what 'Vanda' means?" she asked. I said, "No." And she told me, "In India, 'Vanda' means *Praise to God.*"

So, in spite of my parents' hatred, and all of the rejection, God still brought this name forth for me! Amazing! God makes no mistakes!

Rejection gives you direction. During the time I was growing up and was being kicked around and looked upon with resentment, I didn't understand, because I was just a child. My parents were coming from a very dark place, and later God showed me that He had placed me in that family to bring light. The one thing that my parents were challenged to do was to extinguish the light.

During this period in my life, the system rejected me, because my family was dirt poor and lived on the wrong side of the tracks. I grew up in a place called Cheshire, England. It was a wealthy area, quite beautiful, with schools that were well provided for. In the midst of all this opulence, there was one small degraded section where the poor people lived, in government housing, and that's where I was born.

When I went to school, wearing a uniform, just like the other students' uniform, my shoes had holes in them and revealed my poverty. At that time in England, one was either born into wealth or poverty. If you were poor, there was no advancing from that state, monetarily or otherwise. That was another part of the system that, for me, was rejective.

As children, my siblings and I used to fight to see who could get the last piece of bread and the last bit of margarine. We weren't into sharing, simply because we were all starving. At school we had lunches, which were wonderful to us in our state of starvation, and we would go back for seconds or thirds. That again marked us as the poor kids, and we were rejected.

Living with sexual and physical abuse, along with the rejection, was so difficult and degrading that by the time I was fourteen and a half, I ran away from home. I had suffered so severely from rejection that I felt as if I had been fired from God's bow and arrow. Yet when the bow of rejection was pulled back and the arrow released, it flew farther and higher than it might have had it not been for the force of the rejection. As a result, I landed smack dab in the middle of the United States!

The impact of that rejection took me from one country to another. This was an incredibly positive thing. The United States has been a haven for so many people. That's what makes it so wonderful, because rejected people from all over the world have come to these shores. Those who were outcasts because they dared to think past the dogma, or because they were poor and couldn't fit into the system, or for many other reasons, came to the United States of America. The power of their rejection has helped to make this country strong. Many of those who came were searching for a higher, expanded reality. They were the people's rejects but God's strength.

The ultimate rejection is demonstrated by the life of Jesus. When he first spoke in the temple to the Scribes and the Pharisees, he quoted from the book of Isaiah. Instead of recognizing the wonderful wisdom presented to them, the Scribes and the Pharisees wanted to kill him! The force of that rejection caused Jesus to go out where he belonged and teach the people, going down the highways and the byways, not just hobnobbing with the intellectuals nor the narrow-minded religious hierarchy, but taking His love to the people who couldn't even gain access to the synagogue. This is another example of rejective forces causing us to take new directions. God is not religious, never has been, never will be.

And so I came to the United States, thinking that my rejection was a terrible handicap, and yet it brought positive situations into my life. What

are you doing with the rejection in your life? How far back does the rejection go? To your childhood? To a divorce? To a failed business? What are
you carrying that has so much power that it can turn your life around, if
you allow it? Realize that it is a directive force.

There are two kinds of rejection. One is the rejection we attract by
being Light, not necessarily because of anything we have done. When you
are rejected because you bring light, you are going to be placed in the
darkness. Because if you are light, you belong in the darkness. Do you
comprehend this?

The Holy Spirit sent us here so that all the rejective forces of darkness
could come against us as we grow, so that our light would prevail.
Darkness is simply the absence of light, so, you see, our light can dispel
the darkness and overcome it. Don't let your light go out because of
rejection. Darkness does not embrace the light. Nevertheless, no matter
how tiny your flame, in darkness it can be seen for miles around. Think
of a tiny star. It can be perceived only in the darkness. See yourself as
that tiny star.

If you have been sent as light, you will be sent into dark situations. You
will be rejected, and you will be hurt, just *because* you are the Light. Let
your light shine. Rejection should not put your light out, it should make
it brighter. Let the Holy Spirit overflow your spiritual lamp with oil, so
that in the darkest places your light will shine as a beacon—in your family, occupation, or in any situation that allows the transmutation from
darkness to light.

When others are hurting they will come to you, because the pain inside
of you has made you a warm person to be around. The pain and hurt from
the rejection that you have experienced, as you bring up your light, provides warmth and shelter for others. So use your rejection to the utmost.

I had a strange thing happen to me one day at the market. As I took
my place at the checkout counter, I could feel absolute hatred emanating
from the lady checker. She started throwing my cabbages and tomatoes
as though in a fit of anger. I hadn't done anything to rile her. I thought I

had been quite polite. I couldn't imagine why she was acting this way. When I left, I resolved not to go through her line again when next I came to the market.

Yet when I came again, I lined up behind her counter once more, without realizing it. When my turn at the register came, the same thing happened. She was being hateful and throwing my groceries. Again I resolved to avoid her counter in the future..

On my third visit to the market, I noticed long lines at the other checkout stations, but there was a very short line at this lady's. I quickly took my place at the end of one of the long lines. As I stood there, I heard the voice of the Spirit. It said, "What are you doing?"

"Well," I said, "I'm standing over here because that lady hates me."

"Why does she hate you?"

"I don't know. I didn't do anything."

The Spirit said, "You are like a flashlight shining on her darkness and when you go near her, it makes her very uncomfortable. So she doesn't like you. She would reject any light bearers who come through her check stand. But your job is not to run from the darkness but to bring light into the darkness. So take your eggs and tomatoes and let that lady check you out, and bless her with everything in you. Then when you get home, hold her in your meditation and prayer until you feel the work has been done."

I drew a long breath and thought *Oh boy!* But I went over to the lady's station. She was as hostile as ever, but when I left there I was feeling her sorrow. I returned home and did as the Holy Spirit had directed. I realized I had been running from a situation that was uncomfortable. I think we all do that. It is so much easier to be around other people of light, people who love you and are kind and who think the way you do. Yet we need to add light to the darkness, and even though people resent us, we need to work toward setting them free.

I didn't see that lady again for months and had forgotten about the incidents. Then one day as I returned to the market, I stepped up to be checked out, and there she was. Her whole countenance had changed! There was a radiance about her!

She said, "Hi! How are you doing today?" The change was incredible!

We who have been rejected have that kind of light. But we have to absorb the rejection, turn the light on, and stay in prayer and meditation in order to change people. We can't do it by running away. Of course there are some who resist the light and refuse to change. But this lady just shone! She was precious and so beautiful!

I was thrilled, but also ashamed of myself, because I had tried to run away. Lord knows, I'd had enough rejection in my life to know that it is the overcoming which brings light and hope to others. That only love in its pristine process can give freedom to another as she is wafted to a higher, expanded reality.

Another discovery I made in coming to the United States was that at times I found it more comfortable to be rejected than to be loved. Isn't that strange? You see, when you grow up with rejection, whether verbal or physical, or unspoken, it becomes the familiar. And so when I first came to this country, I wore funny clothes and did strange things to allow people to reject me. I felt it was easier to walk in rejection than it was to be loved. Because love entails responsibility. When you are rejected, you don't have any responsibility. Also, to allow yourself to be loved is to challenge the unfamiliar, and it is difficult to adjust to.

Many of you have learned this lesson, too. As you go through trying marriages or relationships, unpleasant job situations, or business failures, you see yourself as a victim instead of as light. When you have suffered too many hurts, you put up a shield to protect yourself. You are afraid to marry or to be involved, in depth, with your children, or with business associates, because you don't want to be hurt again.

Yet rejection can give you new direction. You just have to use it properly. You need to ask yourself, did I cause the rejection or did it occur because of my light? Let the Holy Spirit give you guidance and perception as to how to respond.

During the first part of my life, I think I used rejection as a crutch. The things that had happened to me as a child became my scapegoat. Then one day I heard the Holy Spirit tell me, "Quit using your hardships as a crutch and start using them as a scepter!" If you will, you can change your own inner being by sweeping your mind with the broom of prayer and meditation, and then you can help many others to achieve the same. Hold your rejective forces high so they can give you new direction.

Remember what trials Jesus went through, over and over again, even to the cross. There was a lot of love received, but also a tremendous amount of rejection. He was called the son of the devil and other demeaning labels, and all he did in return was to spread love. So rejection is a part of our training. Use it as a scepter. Hold up your light so that others will be drawn to it.

Some people are not going to believe what you've experienced in life unless you are willing to share some of your fire time! When you do, you will attract people who are hurting and will be able to help them immensely.

When I had my television ministry, a particular station wanted to buy my series. They would have paid me a large sum of money; and I was greatly excited, because I thought I would no longer have to live in poverty. My life would be easy, and yet I would still be doing the work of the Spirit. To my dismay, the station changed their mind. I felt terribly rejected and disappointed.

However, this led me to return, in earnest, to my group ministry. I was helping about 100 people at that time. So instead of deserting them, thinking I was going to make lots of money, I went back into the work with greater dedication and love. The truth is, the call of the Spirit is stronger and much more rewarding than simply making money.

The message for all of us is: Stop holding your rejection inside and letting it fester. It is a power which can be used positively or negatively. Let the Spirit heal, let Him lead, and let Him use you as a vessel for bringing light into all the dark corners of your life.

---▼---

Nothing Is Permanent
Except Change

PART TWO

▼

A NEW YEAR'S HEART

Beginning Again

The theme of this message is: "Let Go of the Old and Bring in the New." So, basically, it is a New Year's message or the tale of a new beginning.

What we are focusing on today is the letting go of our comfort zones. To be able to walk with the Spirit, we must release many of our comfortable plateaus.

One thing we should do is to make sure we are wearing the right shoes for the spiritual journey that's ahead. Our old soft, comfy, spiritual slippers are not going to serve us, because everybody knows the path is sometimes hard and steep. Now, we may not want to let go. We think, "I can do many things, but allow me to have my little comfort zones. God can still use me."

God wants you to release. These areas may be warm and wonderful, but you have to relinquish whatever those comfort zones are, because there is a road ahead that's steep, sometimes stony, and it needs a different pair of spiritual shoes. Sure, you can leave the comfy slippers on, but eventually, like all things, they are going to wear out. So you can put your little foot down and say I'm going to stay right here, or I'm not going to take that chance. But, you see, nothing is constant, except for change.

Nothing is constant except change. This week I was looking at some of the conditions that demonstrate this. One of the avenues I always look to for spiritual confirmation is nature. So I was studying a big old tree outside our window. It loses its leaves once a year. I always hate to see them go, because the tree is so beautiful, but it has to lose its leaves in order to produce new foliage the next year.

The leaves that fall to the ground become the fertilizer or, metaphorically, the manure for the tree to facilitate and utilize for its growth. I know some of you think you can't help anyone else because there's so much manure in your life. I remember the time when I was living in Phoenix and lost all of my worldly possessions. I lost my business, my home, and every material thing that I treasured. Then The Spirit said to me, "Now I can use you." I thought to myself, *You've got to be kidding me. I'm surrounded by manure!* The Spirit said, "It is the manure in your life that will not only help you to grow tall and strong, spiritually but will enable you to help others grow tall and strong through adversity."

I kept thinking, *How can I help anyone? I have no money. I have no home for people to meet in. I have nothing!* Yet the broken, the divorced, those who had gone through bankruptcy—everybody, it seemed, that was in trouble—came to my door shortly after that time, because I had surrendered. I said, okay, if you can use me to help all of these people, I'm willing. It was just a matter of discarding the old fears and the old way of thinking and letting the new come in.

Perhaps, today, you are deciding, I'm staying in my comfort zone because I'm really afraid to get out of it. I don't want others to know what's going on with me. I don't want to let go of worn-out things, because I'll be embarrassed. What will my friends think?

When I lived in Phoenix, we had a large old orange tree in our yard. In the fall, when all the oranges were gone, the tree would become bare. To me, it looked sad and depleted, but there is a time in everyone's life when you are stripped of all your fruit. It doesn't matter how productive you've been—what a great teacher, dancer, lawyer, or parent—if you don't let go when the season demands it, you will get stripped anyway. The reason being: so that you can produce new spiritual fruit.

One year the orange tree had two oranges that stayed on through the frost and into the spring—no leaves, just two oranges. Some of us hold onto our old spiritual stuff like that, and it looks a bit ludicrous. Yet holding onto old fruit pulls the strength out of the tree. The fruit shrivels up anyway, because nature has a way of making us shed everything in our cycle, We have to let go in order to produce new fruit. It is inevitable.

Well, you may say, a divorce isn't very productive. Yet, if the relationship was causing you and others pain, it had to be terminated. I know there are many churches that will disagree with this. Yet the cycle of life removes the old in order to produce new and better conditions for our growth and happiness. It happens all the time.

Take, for instance, our old dog. She sheds her coat once a year. She can't hold onto that coat. It disappears automatically. You can't circumvent the cycle of nature. Those of you who have kitties and dogs know that they shed. It's not that you particularly want them to, and maybe they don't desire it either, but it happens. Like the tree, they release the old to make room for the new. It's a cycle.

Now some of you might say, I'm too old to change. I can't do this, it's too hard for me, I'm stuck in my ways. Well, even old trees shed their leaves. The oldest tree that loses its leaves doesn't stop one day and say, I'm getting too old for this change. It just keeps on happening. That's the cycle. You must release the old in order to produce the new. Let go of it totally. If you refuse to do it, then God will do it for you.

I remember when I first arrived in Payson, I wanted to have apples and pear trees, and so I bought a small apple tree. I planted it, and after I planted it the Spirit said to me, *prune it!* And I thought, shoot, it's so tiny I don't want to do that. So I left it and went to bed. I woke up in the morning to some weird sounds. I looked out and saw this big, fat, old cow chewing on the tree. And I thought, oh my gosh! My poor tree! And the Spirit said to me, "I said to you, 'prune it.'"

So you see, if you don't allow it to occur, the pruning will happen anyway, and maybe in a way you don't want it to. There are new things that are coming to you, but you must release all your old fruit. No matter how great it seemed, in retrospect, no matter how prolific you were in business, or how successful you were at what you did, don't be afraid to release so that you can produce more fruit.

Old thinking has to go. It's to be relinquished. You can't keep your outdated ways of thinking and expect to grow. It doesn't happen.

When I first arrived in Payson, I wanted to give a gift of some kind to all my neighbors in Beaver Valley, just to get to know them. So I did that, but there was one dear man up the hill—I'll call him Paul—whom everyone warned me about: "Vanda, don't get around Paul, because he likes girls, and you just don't need to be alone with him." So my city thinking clicks in, and I tell myself, *I'm going to stay far away from this guy.* And the Spirit says, "Make him a pie." I thought this was strange, considering his reputation.

I didn't want to make him a pie, and I didn't have anything to make a pie with; but it was blackberry season, so to be obedient, I went out and picked some blackberries. It takes me hours to make a pie from scratch! I looked out the window, thinking that this is why the old-fashioned women and men were so spiritual. It took them so long to accomplish tasks that they couldn't help but think on spiritual things. You know, it took me all morning to make that pie!

Yet I baked it and I took it up to him, and I said, "Paul I'm new in the neighborhood, and I felt I would really like to make you this pie. I just felt that I was supposed to do this, just to kind of get to know you."

He said, "Would you like to come in?" I stepped back and said, "Oh no, thank you." And I went quickly back to my house.

A couple of days later he was driving by, and he said, "Do you realize it's getting very cold? You're going to need some wood."

We had a big old wood stove in our house, and I didn't even know how it worked. I said, "Oh there's lots of wood in the field, I don't really need any."

He said, "No, Honey, you're going to need some wood. It snows up here."

Coming from Phoenix, I couldn't vision *snow*. I said, "Oh, I can always pick up scraps of wood around the property."

He said, "Well, listen, if you would like, I'll take you out in the woods, and we can get some firewood."

My city thinking said definitely, *No!* And so I said, "Thank you. That's really nice of you, but I'll be fine."

So the weather kept getting colder and colder. One day I was praying and I said, "I guess I need some wood." And the Spirit said to me, "You've been offered wood." And I thought, *Oh, my gosh!* And He said, "I want you to accept it." And I almost panicked, but the next time Paul offered, I said, "Okay, thank you. I'll go get wood with you."

So we went driving out into the woods. Paul was in his seventies but very spry and in super shape. He had his old wood-hauling truck, and he said to me, "I'll cut and you put it on the truck."

So I loaded all this wood onto the truck, and my back was killing me! Even though he's twice my age, he was cutting away and telling me all about the different kinds of timber. While we worked he asked me about my beliefs. He had heard of my ministry. He called me preacher woman. That's what the neighbors used to call me there in Beaver Valley.

I started to share some spiritual insights with him, just simple things that had happened in my life. And, you know, a couple of times his eyes became misty. And I thought, *I'm such an unkind person, sometimes I judge so easily, and my negative thinking really can hurt what the Spirit is trying to do in my life.*

Later, when we pulled into my driveway with our load, I expected him to give me half the wood, but he said, "Well, Honey, this wood's for you."

I thought, *Gosh! All of it?* Then it occurred to me that I would have to unload it! But he presses this little button on his old wood truck; the back end goes up and all the wood drops into a pile. It was fantastic! I almost reached over and gave him a hug, but I wasn't quite that brave, so I simply thanked him.

When he was gone, I went into the house and fixed a cup of tea and thought, *I'm hurting!* Every bone in my body ached. I was sitting down, sipping my tea, when the Spirit said one more thing to me that night: "Go stack it." And I thought, *Noooo! Why? I'm too tired and I hurt!*

Do you ever wonder why you are sometimes led in directions you don't want to go? It may seem weird, yet you know deep inside you that are supposed to follow the prodding. Well, I got up and put my shoes on and went outside. There was a *cord* of wood to be stacked under the eaves! The task seemed insurmountable!

Nevertheless, I started stacking the wood and wondering what the heck I was doing. I felt that maybe it was my punishment for having had such bad thoughts about this man. When, at last, it was all stacked up, I went inside and fell into bed. I was aching! But I went to sleep, and it was probably the best night's sleep I ever had. I woke up at ten o'clock in the morning, and when I looked outside, there was snow everywhere! There hadn't been any forecast of snow, but the Spirit knew. My wood was dry, because I followed the Spirit.

Had I not changed my old way of thinking, I would have missed one of my greatest blessings. It was not just receiving the wood, not only seeing the miracle—the sudden change from a sunny day to winter and knowing I was prepared—but being able to enjoy this man I had feared, who really was very precious. Through my old way of thinking, I had learned to judge people according to what others were saying , and so I nearly missed this wonderful experience.

We need to release all of our old thinking and the archaic stuff in our lives. How many of us have a garage that barely has room for the car? We collect things, don't we?

When we go backpacking, for instance, we put on our backpack and immediately start collecting things. I collect rocks, and feathers, and all kinds of objects. In everyday life we do that too. We collect a lot of emotional junk that's not necessary. As we go along on our life's journey, if we're traveling toward a higher spiritual level, we're going to find that we need to detach from a lot of the old garbage that we've carried for eons.

Some of you who are on a spiritual path are carrying a lot of unnecessary stuff on your back—in your spiritual backpack—that is a hindrance to you. There are some ancient lovers in your pack that remind you of old hurts and misunderstandings. There are feelings of past pain, of low self-worth, of unforgiveness, and of guilt. Each time you try to take a step forward, the heaviness that you are carrying on your back slows you down and limits your progress.

Unless you release the burdens of the past, there will be no room in your spiritual backpack for the new. You must let go of all the pain and sorrows so that you can fill your pack with new treasures that will provide happy memories and allow you to walk with a lighter step.

Who didn't pay a debt owed to you? Does it matter? It makes your load lighter if you forgive. The higher you rise in the Spirit, the less stuff you need to carry. The higher up the spiritual mountain you go, the fewer possessions you will need. Your breathing will change as you climb higher. The air will become cleaner. Yet you may have fewer friends, because as you ascend the mountain you will meet fewer people. As your pack gets lighter, you may also find that you have left many friends behind. Not everyone has the courage or the aspiration to progress spiritually.

Don't be afraid to conquer. If you are worried about your children, or your husband, wife, or friends, realize that you cannot carry them and yourself too. You must go ahead and hope they will follow, but you can't carry them. The higher up you go, the lighter must be your load. The higher you climb, the less you need. Fewer people will be with you, because many can't keep up with you or your thinking. Neither will they understand why you have changed your old comfy spiritual slippers for hiking shoes, for shoes that are strong and sensible. Nor will they understand why you have traveled to places that are sometimes very, very lonely.

Do your best to liberate yourself from the old so that you can experience the new. Whether it's wrong thinking, clinging to past situations, or lack of forgiveness—whatever is hindering you—release. Surrender the old hurts, the agonizing mental pain, the unforgiveness. You cannot travel to the higher places if you're carrying the lower vibrational emotions, such as hate, anger, judgment, or jealousy. If your upward climb is hindered by them, you must relinquish your old comfort zones.

Banish your judgments and your erroneous thinking and get yourself in line with the Spirit.

Father, Mother God, we thank you, because you are always with us. You carry us when we can walk no farther. You lighten our load by removing that which we shouldn't be carrying . Teach us not to hold onto our old encumbrances. Remind us to observe how nature reincarnates every year. Help us to be one with Your Spirit, to take a chance, to let go, to take another chance and another step upward.

Help us not to grieve over the old loves and the old friends and the things that belong to the past. Let us hold hands with anyone who might be on the same path for a time, but give us the courage to go on alone when the trail gets too narrow for two. Thank you for your love that fills us. Thank you for the wind of the Spirit, which whispers wisdom and fresh thoughts. Help us to forgive ourselves and to release the things that drag us down.

And so it is.

---▼---

An Empty Heart Has Great Potential To Be Filled

PART THREE

▼

A VALENTINE HEART

Finding Your Soul Mate

When we think of Valentine's Day, we think of being filled with love. I've heard so many people say that they wish they always could be filled with God's love and do good deeds. Yet to express this kind of love on a daily basis is not easy. I have pondered on why we find it so difficult to be filled with love and compassion.

One of the reasons that occurred to me is this: You cannot fill a vessel that is already full. In order for God to fill us with love, we first have to spiritually empty ourselves . We must trust the hands of the Holy Spirit to tip our life just a little bit and let the stale water pour out.

Many of us don't wish to let this happen, because it leaves us feeling naked. It's as though we've suddenly become as transparent as a glass bottle. We don't like to feel that people can see through us, and so we don't want to allow all the old garbage to go. Yet if we wish to be filled to capacity with God's love, we first have to make room. We must empty ourselves.

This is a difficult task, because the more others can see through us, the more vulnerable we feel.

However, it only makes good sense that if you want to have a clean body, you have to cleanse yourself, spiritually, mentally, and physically. You take vitamins and herbs; some people fast; you try to get yourself in shape. You do whatever is necessary to get yourself clean inside and out. That's how you heal, by getting rid of all the rubbish in your life. Sometimes the Holy Spirit helps by taking a wire brush and scrubbing you from the inside out. It may be painful, or it may hurt your pride, but you can't say that you want to be filled with God's love if you're not willing to be cleansed.

Remember when the Master Jesus said that you can't put new wine in old wine skins? Why? Because the new wine expands and will burst the container. Now, I don't know about you, but I want to be filled to capacity with God's love, but I certainly don't want to burst! So I realize I must be cleaned out first…

I've gone through many physical fasts, having been directed by the Spirit, and have spent much time on this process; but I find it needs to be done, not just one time but many times. Following the cleansing, there is usually a major shift that takes place, a shift in consciousness as well as in physical well-being.

We need to look within ourselves. We have to rid ourselves of the burdens we carry around with us, grief, for instance. Many of us are carrying so much grief we find it difficult to go on with life. We have to be able to say, "Holy Spirit, I'm hurting inside, and I need you to remove the grief." Whether it's because a loved one has gone to the other side, whether it's a broken relationship, or that our children have left us, whatever the situation is, we need to be able to abandon the grief.

We have to let go of divorce situations, bankruptcies, and other embarrassing circumstances. There are also some happy experiences that we need to release, and that's very hard to do. For instance, we sometimes wish that we could go back to being a child, because life seemed so much easier then. We wish things were the way we remember them in our childhood, when others took care of us. We feel it is too hard being an adult; it is too painful. But we have to mature.

Life is a school, and each time we graduate from one level, we come into a higher grade of living, a higher place in the spirit. We have to allow that graduation to take place. If we fail the first test, it is going to present itself to us again. If we dislike Joe down the street, believe me, the Holy Spirit has another hundred Joe's to bring our way, just to give us the opportunity to overcome. We have to release our judgments. We must learn to love.

People say that there are certain medical conditions that cause cancer or that cause heart attacks, but there's a physical and a spiritual aspect to that. Have you ever heard someone say that so-and-so died of a broken heart? It happens when we can't get on with life because we are unable to overcome grief and depression.

In England the boys and the girls are usually in different schools. The boys have to wear short pants with suspenders, school tie, and little hats. When they get to be around fourteen or fifteen, with hairy legs, they look so comical! Because they are too mature to wear little boys' clothes.

Sometimes we are like those young boys, wearing our costumes of the past, which we haven't been able to let go. We look pretty silly, spiritually, when we won't detach from the past and let the Holy Spirit do the cleansing. We can't hold onto the past. We can't return to our childhood. We can't be preoccupied with old hurts, either, because the pain causes physical as well as spiritual illnesses. The Holy Spirit wants to cleanse us and prepare us to be filled with the new wine of love.

Now we need to surrender to the Spirit. He's like a master surgeon. He's not going to force anybody to relinquish their pain. Neither is He going to start cutting on anybody, emotionally. He waits for us to say, "Holy Spirit, come. I'll take a little heart surgery. I'm ready for this process. I'll let go of the pain. I'll release the unforgiveness, the hatred, and the anger. Because I really do want to be overflowing with this love."

Once you've given the Spirit permission and said *I'm ready,* know that your life is going to turn upside down, because it tends to do that! He doesn't take you lightly at your word.

One time the Master Jesus saw a man sitting by the pool. He was sick, and so his friends had brought him there every day in hopes of a healing. The Master asked, "Do you want to be made well?" Now why would he ask him if he *wanted* to be made well when He knew the man had been coming every day, hoping to be healed?

There are people who don't want to give up their yesterdays or their pain. It is their crutch. Sometimes it's hard to let go and say, "Yes, I do want to be healed." Because, having the sickness—whether it's physical or spiritual or both—gives you an excuse to stay in that same plane, the one that is familiar.

So the Holy Spirit will check with you and ask, "Do you really want to be healed? Do you really want me to take all this emotional junk away so I can fill you with love? Or are you happy with your present state? Are you happy being forlorn? Are you content having this misery inside of you?"

When he asks you, you need to be very truthful. Are you really ready to move on? Are you ready to release your old stuff? Can you give up your good experiences too?

Often when others are being kind to us we feel we are not deserving. We tend to think that we don't rate such kindness. Or if someone is yelling at us and saying nasty and hurtful words, something rises up in us that wants to feed the image of unworthiness which that person has implied. If we feed that monster, it will get bigger. If we can ignore the words and turn away in love, the monster has to die, because it has no food, no hate to feed upon.

So if you really want this heart surgery, then you must, symbolically, sign the papers with the Holy Spirit and get on with the work. It's not just a matter of saying that you want to be attuned with the love of God. You first have to experience the cleaning-out process.

There is a magnet within you, a spiritual magnet, that vibrates, either at a low or high rate, and attracts people of that vibratory rate. So you need to raise your vibrations to the level of those whom you wish to attract. As you work on yourself, you will draw to you people that will be in harmony with you, your values, and your goals.

There are machines that can test a person's vibratory rate. When you spend time in prayer and meditation, the increase in your vibrations will register on these machines. So, you see, it has been proven that people can consciously raise their electrical frequency. If you are looking for friends, or someone to love, or for your life to change, you can change your magnetic vibrations to bring the right people or situations into your life by attuning yourself to the cosmic clock of creation.

I can testify that this really works. When I was in England, my husband David was in the United States. I hadn't met him yet, perhaps because we were not vibrating at the same rate. At that time I was not yet a loving, caring person. I was still going through my growth and my clearing. Later I came to the United States, and at one time we were both living in Phoenix just a few streets away from one another. We lived within a close proximity to each other for two years without meeting.

Then I moved to the little town of Payson. I wasn't looking for a husband at that time. I was involved with becoming whole and integrated within myself and with the spiritual work I was dedicated to.

I had a group of about 50 or 60 people meeting at my home every Saturday night whom I was ministering to, trying to help them with their lives, and I was growing with them. Many of the people brought their teenage children. David walked into the meeting one day and asked, "Do you have someone who can work with the young people?" I told him no, that we had been praying for such a person, and he replied, "I would like to do that for the group."

After we had worked together for six months, the Holy Spirit began to attune David and me and told us that we were to be married. We hadn't dated at that point, but I started to look at him as a prospective husband.

Neither of us had been looking for a mate, and David wasn't sure that the message we had received came from the Holy Spirit, so he said, "If this really came from the Holy Spirit, I'm going to need some proof."

When David wants to find spiritual answers, he goes hiking. So he put on his backpack and hiked into the woods for a couple of days. When he returned he said, "Okay. I have a scripture in my pocket, and if you're to be my wife you'll know what that scripture is."

I looked at him and said, rather sarcastically, "Well, that's really wonderful, but I haven't been given a scripture—unless it's about washing the disciples' feet or something like that." And he said, "That's it!" He brought a piece of paper out of his pocket, and on that paper was written the scripture about washing the disciples' feet!

What the Holy Spirit was telling us was that from that day forth we were to serve one another in marriage and in love. That was on Thanksgiving, and we decided to get married on Christmas Day.

During that interval I had a dream in which I saw a ring. It had inscribed on it "Love never fails", and it had a cross on it. I woke up and wondered, what am I supposed to do about this? There was one small jewelry shop in town, and I decided to go there and see if they could make this ring. I walked into the little shop, feeling a bit embarrassed, because David hadn't said anything about a ring yet. I was sketching a picture of the ring when someone entered the shop. I turned around, and it was David! He had been given the exact same vision for his ring and my ring!

We have now been married nine years, and he is the most wonderful person I have ever known.

That's my valentine story. It came about because we were vibrating on the same level by the time we were drawn together. So, you see, if you will allow the synchronization, your vibrations are going to attract someone of like vibrations.

There was a gentleman on the Oprah Winfrey show some time ago. He had been in a concentration camp in Poland. He was nineteen then. He said that every day during that time a little girl, thirteen years old, would come by and hand him her apple through the fence. She rarely said anything except, "I know you're hungry." For two years her love and her apples kept him alive.

One day when she came by, he told her, "Don't come any more. They are going to move me to another place." Although he didn't tell her so, he thought that he was going to the death camp. She tearfully agreed not to come. Twenty years later, after surviving the war, this man was living in the United States. One day a friend of his invited him to dinner and told him that he would like for him to meet a friend.

The man and his friend took a cab and picked up the lady. When she got into the cab, he looked into her eyes and recognized the little girl who had saved his life! He asked, "Do you remember ever having given me an apple?" Before she could even answer, he asked her, "Will you marry me?" And, of course, she did, because they were so perfectly attuned to the cosmic rhythm.

How can we not believe that the Holy Spirit will bring two people together if it is meant to be? I love that story. God is incredible in the way He moves in His pristine uniqueness.

If you have been searching, if you have been going through a grieving process, know that the Spirit cares about you. All He wishes to do is to purify you and help you get on your feet. If you let Him, He will bring to you the people or the situations that you need to fulfill your life.

Author Bernie Seigel gives us this little tip. He says, "Marry yourself first." *Marry yourself first.* I'll let you figure it out.

We must be filled with the Spirit in order to rise above whatever situation we are in so that we can see the whole picture. We can't see the whole picture while we're down. We have to raise our consciousness so that we can see the divine plan as a jigsaw puzzle and realize that, in it, we all fit together. It doesn't matter how large or small we are, what color our skin is, or what color our hair is. Everybody fits into the picture in the divine template of existence. It's merely a matter of finding our place. Once we are emptied out and filled with love, we will know where that place is.

BALANCE—HURRY UP AND SLOW DOWN

PART FOUR

▼

BALANCE OF THE HEART

Balancing the Impossible

Finding mental and physical balance in our lives can sometimes be a stormy process. Often things are taken away from us in order to balance us. While I was meditating on this one day, my whole body suddenly went out of balance. I thought, well this is different. There must be a reason for this.

It occurred to me that I had boasted that week that I never get sick. You know what happens to people with pride, don't you? Well, here I was, sick, and trying to find out what God was trying to tell me. I know that being in balance physically depends on one's being in balance mentally and spiritually. Balance is very important.

When I was a little girl, about seven or eight, my grandma was trying to teach me to ride a bicycle. It looked huge to me. Grandma said to me, "Now, Vanda, if you just look straight ahead and don't look down at the ground and just pedal forward, you'll be able to ride. The only problem was, my grandma never let go of the seat! She kept telling me, "You can do it," but she held onto that seat so tightly that I couldn't ride the bicycle, because I wasn't able to get my balance. She was so afraid to let go.

I think a lot of us are like that in our relationships with our husbands, our wives, our children, and our grandchildren. We find it very, very difficult to let go and let God. Yet until my grandmother released that bicycle seat, I was going nowhere. When she did, I fell many times. I skinned my knees and bruised my elbows, but I learned to get back on that bike and ride like the wind. Yet it wasn't until *she let go.*

Many of us are holding onto situations or relationships too tightly. Persons that we love can't progress, because we're affecting their balance. I've done this with both my daughters. Figuratively speaking, I still grab the back of their bicycle seat at times, because I love them so much and I'm afraid they're going to be hurt. Yet sometimes the only way they learn balance is by falling. My children have fallen so frequently that I have to keep reminding myself not to say, *I told you so.* Instead, I try to cheer them on.

When a baby is learning to walk and falls down, we clap and tell him *that's wonderful,* and the little tot gets up and starts going again. He's learning how to balance, just as we are learning how to balance our lives.

One of my favorite people in the Bible is Peter. Peter had a propensity for saying things he probably wished he hadn't. I can identify with that. Do you remember the story in Matthew when Peter is on the boat with the Disciples and there's a raging storm with huge waves? It was about 4:00 o'clock in the morning, and Jesus came to them, walking on the water. The Disciples screamed in terror, because they thought he was a ghost. But Jesus spoke to them reassuringly and told them not to be afraid.

Peter called to Jesus and said, "Lord, if it is you, bid me come to you on the water." He really put his foot in his mouth, didn't he! But Jesus told him, "Come." Peter went over the side of the boat and walked on the water toward Jesus, but because of the force of the wind and the waves—but more importantly, because Peter took his eyes off Jesus and looked at the waves of circumstances—he was afraid and began to sink. He cried, "Lord, save me!" Jesus immediately held out his hand and rescued Peter. "O man of little faith," Jesus said, "Why did you doubt?"

How many times have you gone over the side of the boat? I've done it over and over, because I was so eager to get out there and do something challenging or different. We've all done it. We think, Oh, I can do it! But then we look at the waves of circumstances around us and we start to wonder. What are people going to think? What if I can't pay for it? What if I fail? What if? What if? These waves around us become overwhelming and cause us to lose our balance.

Yet when the huge storms come into our lives, and the waves throw us left and right, we emerge to discover that we are more balanced. We discover, too, that we have ended up where we are supposed to be.

When you are surrounded by frightening circumstances, you've got to keep your eye on the goal or on whatever master you put your faith into. Keep your focus on the outcome you are striving for. Don't look at the waves that surround you, for if you do you will sink. Of course the Holy Spirit will be there to pick you up, but you might feel like a bit of a fool. Don't we all?

The thing is, Jesus loved Peter, because, although he had a big mouth, he also had a big heart. I think that is what He is looking for from us. When faced with a challenge, just have the heart to say, "Yes. I will. I'll do it. No matter how hard it is, no matter how frightening, no matter how big the waves are around me, I'm going to go out there and do it." He'll always go with you and pick you up if you need Him to.

Peter may have looked foolish in front of his friends as he started to sink. Maybe there was a bit of pride involved, too. Peter may have had an urge to show off a little when he asked Jesus to request that he walk on the water to him while all the Disciples were watching. Then down he went!

Sometimes pride enters in when we set out to do something, and perhaps we forget whether we are doing it for God or doing it for ourselves. When we get caught up in an endeavor, we should ask ourselves, "Am I doing this for God or for me?" We need to keep things in perspective and in balance.

Balance is so important in all of life, in one's spiritual walk, in one's personal affairs, in one's finances. My husband and I have been talking about balancing our finances. We decided that we needed to get rid of all of our credit cards. Before we went up to Flagstaff recently, I had one credit card in my wallet just for emergencies. As I was getting ready to leave, the Holy Spirit said to me, "Why do you have a credit card for emergencies? What did you do before, when you couldn't even qualify for credit?"

I thought, God, I trusted you with all my heart. Whatever I needed, I prayed for, because I didn't have a choice." Even if I wanted to give someone a gift, I prayed, "God, I really want to do this. Please provide it for me." He would, if it was the right thing to do. Yet I think that sometimes I've bought gifts on my credit card when it really wasn't appropriate. But I didn't pray and I didn't wait. I just charged it.

There was a time when I started a spiritual group. At first there were just twelve people, but it later grew to over two hundred. These people were very special to me. I was barely scraping a living at the time when there were just twelve in the group, but I really wanted to give them a Christmas present, and I prayed to God to help me find a way. There was a little inspirational book that cost about $8.00 that I wanted to give to each of them. I kept praying and praying and telling God how much I wanted to do this. Christmas kept getting closer and closer, with no resolution.

One day, a member of the group came to me and handed me a gift. He told me that I needed to open it before Christmas. So I unwrapped it. It was a photograph album. I said, "Thank you very much." He told me, "I want you to open it." Then he said, "I think, if I was hearing from The Spirit, it is right on the nose." So I opened the album, and on each page was $8.00. There were twelve pages!

God really, really cares for us. We don't need credit cards. We don't need other avenues for our provision. He is all we need. So now, instead of a credit card in my wallet, I carry a little card in it that says "Pray." Because

I used to pray all the time but had become so focused on worldly things, it caused me to become unbalanced. I had been using my credit card instead of a prayer card.

There was another situation when I bought a family a whole Thanksgiving dinner, then used the credit card to get us through the month. I felt quite justified. Later I learned that I had deprived someone else of that opportunity to give.

We just don't know. We have to wait. We have to pray. We have to stay in balance. I'm not telling anyone to throw away your credit cards. Everybody's walk is different. Everybody's truth is different. That's what makes humanity so balanced as a unit.

There's a little story I like to tell to illustrate this. A little boy was with his daddy. There was a circus going by. His daddy was looking over the fence, but the boy was too small to see over it, so he found a hole in the fence to look through. His daddy said, "Look, look, Son! Do you see the elephant?" The boy said, "No, Daddy." "Well, look again," his dad said, "Can't you see an elephant?" The boy repeated, "No, Daddy." The father asked, "What's wrong with you? It's right there. Can't you see the elephant?" His son said, "No, Daddy. All I can see is a patch of gray."

Whose is the right truth? The father's, or the little boy's? Where's the balance? The thing is, both were right; both were totally correct. Both had seen the same thing, just in a different perspective or under different circumstances.

Don't judge others when they seem a bit off balance to you. Metaphorically, lift them up on your shoulders, as the daddy did with the little boy. He lifted him up and said, "See, Son. There, now you're up higher. You can see."

What God does for us by the power of His spirit, when we pray and ask for balance, is to lift us up so that we can see the whole picture instead of just a small amount of truth.

We are not to judge one another. One person's path is not necessarily the same as another's. The way one person dresses is not the same as the way another person dresses. We all have feet but do not have the same shoe size. That is what makes each of us unique.

It's like a jigsaw puzzle with all the little pieces. You pick up one and wonder where the heck does this go? It seems so small that it doesn't fit in. Sometimes I feel too small to fit in. Yet each piece is necessary in order to complete the whole picture. So when you are feeling down and think you are unimportant, realize that without you the whole picture of God's creations would not be complete.

You are as important in the balance of creation as anyone else. A little piece of a jigsaw puzzle is just as necessary to complete the picture as a large piece. A black one is no different than a white one, just so long as they all fit together. So don't mind if you feel pushed at times because someone is being fitted in next to you. You may think you want to be alone, but you can't fit into the big picture unless you let this process happen.

We need to let the wind of the Spirit fill our sails and blow us where it will. We often tie ourselves down with our material possessions. Yet balance is found in letting God fill your sails, take you through the storms, and let you land where you are supposed to be.

Look at Christopher Columbus. He discovered America by mistake. Although everybody told him the world was flat, he knew that if he put his faith in God he could keep on sailing and would not be deterred. He prayed every day that God would take care of him and his crew. When it appeared he would lose his life and his men, that ship's sails filled with the wind, and though tossed by waves, landed on these great shores. Because he allowed God to fill his sails, he weathered the storms.

When you feel the storms of life are raging and you don't know where you're going, just look at the wind and think about the seeds it is scattering. They wouldn't get scattered if the days were all calm and tranquil. When you are scattered by stormy winds, your essence takes root and produces fruit in many different places.

So perceive your storms as blessings. Know that if every day were sunny, there would be no growth. Thank God for balancing you by giving you both rain and sunshine in your lives so that you can grow.

Paramahansa Yogananda tells a story about a Rama who went to the mountains of India to be taught how to become a highly spiritual man. He started his mission enthusiastically, because he had a great desire to become a holy man. His teacher told him that if he performed the duties shown him he would become holy. The first day he had to sweep the roads and other menial tasks. This irritated the man. It was not what he had anticipated. He wanted to be taught, not to be assigned to drudging labor.

By the end of the first six months, the would-be holy man had had enough of it. He went to his teacher and told him that he was not receiving the lessons he had expected and wanted to go out and explore on his own. He planned to take just a little begging bowl and two loin cloths and go into the Himalayas where he felt he could truly become holy. The wise master let him go on his way.

So the man went into the mountains. The first night he hung one of his loin cloths in a tree and went to sleep. The next morning he found that a monkey had taken his begging bowl, and a mouse had bitten holes through the loin cloth in the tree.

The man took his anger out on God. He said, "God, I put all my trust in you and look what you've done to me!" While he was sitting there feeling sorry for himself, a villager came by and asked him what was the matter. He told him about the mouse having eaten his loin cloth. So the villager went home and returned with a cat. He presented the cat to the holy man and said, "Now you won't have to worry about the mice."

The man thanked him. Every day he went into the village for milk for the kitty. The villagers soon tired of this and gave the man a cow. However, the cow started ravaging the villagers' fields and causing trouble. The villagers were becoming resentful, but they went to the man and said, "Holy Man, we have decided to give you 25 acres of land for your cow.

The man gratefully accepted the land, but then he began to bully the village children into taking care of the land, the cow, and the cat. The villagers were even more distressed, and so the head villager went to see the holy man and told him he would give him his eldest daughter so that he could marry and have children of his own to do his work.

The man's master teacher, through his intuition, learned about the situation and went to see the self-proclaimed holy man. He asked him if he would like to come back to the hermitage and learn how to be holy. "Ah, yes!" said the man. That's balance.

Mother/Father God, Thank you for the love that is around us at all times. Thank you for keeping us in balance and for balancing the earth. For allowing her to quake or to use whatever means is necessary to stabilize herself. Let us do the same. Help us to stay in balance so that we can move in harmony with nature and with you, that we can become one with you. Let us remember to allow other people their truths. Help us to let go of memories of past incidents that cause us to be unbalanced. Let your balance flow through our hearts so that we can be all that we were meant to be. Amen.

SPEAK LOUDLY WITH SILENCE

▼

PART FIVE

HARMONY OF THE HEART

Balancing the Emotions

When I think of harmony, I think of music. I think of notes and a cosmic rhythm. I think of people coming together, blending together. I think of a meaningful relationship between a man and a woman. When I consider how different we all are, I realize how wonderful it is when people can merge harmoniously and form a union. If all of us can unite as a cosmic family, we can make a beautiful symphony.

This morning about six o'clock, I was in my little washroom meditating. I had been in there for quite some time and was beginning to feel uplifted but a bit tense. I heard my husband upstairs working with the audio equipment. He was testing it to see if it worked. Now, when I test the equipment, I say: "Testing, one, two, three." But when he was testing it, he said, "Yo, ho, ho, and a bottle of rum!" I started laughing, and I realized that I had to lighten up in order to get what God was saying. He knows that the blending of our differences is what provides the balance.

So many times ladies say of their husbands, "He's just not in the least bit spiritual." Often you hear men say of their wives, "She's always up in the clouds. I just don't know where she is." Yet it is the blending of the male and female qualities which produces harmony. Each complements the other.

Ladies, we need to be grounded, and our mate is grounding us. For the male spirit always grounds, and it is to our advantage if we can embrace it instead of fighting it all of the time.

These were some of the things that came to me this morning, after my husband gave me a good laugh. What I was receiving was that we shouldn't be separate. We need to be blended together.

We can sing a scale—do, re, mi, fa, so la, ti, do—and when the notes blend together, we get beautiful harmony. If we were all do's, we could not create a melody. If we were all re's, the music would be boring. We have to harmonize to create a oneness. Everyone's note is needed to make a tune. No matter how unimportant you think you are, know that every single person is essential in order to create the harmony, the melody of life.

You can't create a beautiful symphony if there's even one note missing. We are all instruments of God. Ladies, you may think: Well, I'm not a very significant instrument. I don't do much. I just love my husband and take care of the house. Yet, you do not know how many people you have supported or inspired.

So every little part that we play is necessary to create the symphony. It's really, really important that everybody plays their notes, their part. Don't try to make somebody a *do* if they're a *re*, or make them a *la* if they're a *ti*. Because we mustn't judge. Every vibration is needed for the cosmic symphony of life in order to bring perfectly attuned rhythm as we tune out all discord!

Timing is a part of harmony. How do you know what the correct timing is when you are considering an action? When you're moving out of the cosmic timing, the harmony is disrupted. In order to move into the proper timing, you have to listen first. Be still and listen to what God is saying and then act on it. To be attuned, we must be willing to close off our speculation and synchronize with the melodious voice of the Spirit.

Sometimes it involves a very simple act. Yesterday I was in my little cubbyhole meditating. In the midst of the spiritual guidance I was receiving came the words, "Call the cleaners." I thought that was a silly thought so tried to ignore it. However, when I heard it again I decided I'd better do it. I called the cleaners and asked if my dress was ready. I knew that it was, but I've learned over the years to follow my guidance. The lady said, "Yes, it's ready, but did you know we are closing in ten minutes.?" I didn't know that, and I had to have the dress that day!

It was just a simple thing, but it is the simple as well as the important events that the Holy Spirit will guide us in, if we would just listen and follow.

Two weeks ago, my daughter Vanessa, my grandson, and I were driving up the hill to Payson from Phoenix. It was about ten o'clock at night. Now I believe I still have a great deal of work to do on the earth, and I also believe that both Vanessa and our little grandson have a great calling in their lives too. I was driving my husband's big Dodge Ram truck. I had it on cruise control at the speed limit. It was quite dark. The baby was fussy, and I was eager to get home. I suddenly heard the Spirit tell me, "Pray the prayer of protection and put that protection around you and the children. Use the prayer of protection."

I was given a word, which has a lot of different vibrations in it. It is a special word that some use to pray when danger is coming. Although I had no idea why I was doing this—except that I knew we have to listen and move when the Spirit speaks—I began to pray. Five minutes later our headlights picked up an elk standing in the middle of the highway. There was no time to stop. We tried to swerve, but as we swerved so did she. As we hit her, she landed right on top the hood. Had we not swerved, however, she would have come through the windshield, as we had been driving at 55 miles an hour. She weighed several hundred pounds!

We pulled off the road. Vanessa and I and the baby all started scream-ing. We knew that had the elk come through the windshield we all would have been killed. The elk was sitting in the ditch. We ran to her to see how badly she was hurt, as the front end of our truck was totally smashed. She seemed dazed, but we saw no blood. To our amazement, she suddenly jumped up and started running.

Then my focus shifted to the truck. What was I going to tell my hus-band? He loved his truck! But then the Holy Spirit said, "Remember what I told you five minutes before the accident? Indeed you would have been killed, but because you listened and were cautious, three lives have been saved."

In order to stay in harmony with the Holy Spirit, you have to listen to what the Spirit is saying. In order to listen you need to sit still and get quiet, no matter how panicked you are, even if you don't understand. So when you hear the voice of the Spirit, you must act upon it.

Have you ever missed attending a meeting, because you didn't really want to go, then after hearing about it wished that you had? Perhaps the Spirit was instructing you to go, but you didn't listen. Many times the most ordinary incident will bring about the most extraordinary effects in your life.

Do you remember the Bible story about Saul when he was asked to go out and find his father's asses? (See 1 Samuel, Ch. 9) Saul was a young, handsome man and no doubt had other things he would rather do, but he listened to his dad and went out looking for the donkeys. In the process of what seemed to be a long and futile search, Saul met Samuel who told him, "The Lord has anointed you to be prince over His heritage."

This meeting opened Saul's heart and changed his life, for by following Samuel's directions Saul was soon hailed as a king. Yet what would have happened had he not listened to his father, Kish, and done as he was asked?

How many times in your life have you thought, "I wish I'd gone, I wish I'd done that," or "I wish I had said good-by"? Sometimes, just before ones I knew had gone over to the other side, I had the feeling I should visit them, or tell them something comforting, or do something special, and I didn't do it because I was too busy. Then I felt as though my heart was going to break, because I hadn't listened and followed the Holy Spirit.

We have to be in harmony with the Spirit all the time, not just some of the time. We need to remind ourselves that if the Holy Spirit tells us to give a dollar or to lend a helping hand to someone, there's a possibility that person may be gone tomorrow. It may be so small a thing we are asked to do that we think it won't matter if we put if off or ignore it.

I remember one time I knew that I was supposed to go visit a friend of mine. I *knew* it, but I didn't do it, because I had a lot of things going on so told myself I would go the following week. When I heard a day or two later that she had passed on, I cried because it was such a simple thing that I had been asked to do. I was led by the Spirit, and I ignored the guidance. So if the Spirit is prodding you, even though the urging seems insignificant, follow. Because when we listen to His instructions and act upon them, we are in harmony with the Holy Spirit.

You are an essential piece of this cosmic order, and it's important to follow the directives. If you are playing a trombone in an orchestra and don't follow the music, then come in at the wrong time, perhaps when the flutes are being featured, aren't you going to feel embarrassed? The soft, delicate melody is going to become distorted, because you are out of harmony. Don't become out of harmony with your life.

One time, years ago, when I lived in Beaver Valley, my children were gone and I was out of groceries, except for a couple of potatoes. I felt I really wanted fish for my supper. I had never gone fishing and didn't know how to catch a fish, so I asked God to help me. I found a stick and tied a line onto it with a hook someone had left at my house, and I went to the river. Feeling totally inept, I kept praying to God to put a fish on my line. Suddenly something started pulling on my line. I reeled it in, and there was a beautiful trout.

Then it was I realized I didn't know what to do with it! I thought, oh-my-gosh, what am I supposed to do now? I think you're supposed to hit it

on the head. I couldn't make myself do it! Killing was not in harmony
with my soul. So I carried it home, while it wriggled on the end of my
line, as I didn't know how to get the hook out of it. By the time I reached
home, the fish was dead.

So I took it in the house and chopped off its head. Then I washed it and
put it in the microwave. After a while it simply exploded! I didn't know
you were supposed to clean it first. There it was, in little fragments all over
my microwave oven. It made me sick. By the time I had scraped it all off
and cleaned up the mess, having delivered the trout to the trash bin, I had
no appetite.

The next morning, when I came back from doing errands, I found a little freezer box on my patio. It had a note on it from my neighbors, telling
me that they had to go to Phoenix and had already defrosted these fish so
couldn't refreeze them, and they hoped I could use them. Inside the freezer
were twelve beautiful fish, all filleted. I ate fish for three days, but I learned
my lesson! When we ask the Holy Spirit for something, He will always
honor the request, but He may teach painful lessons in the process.

I thanked God for the fish and for the lessons, but I realized that I
couldn't go against my own soul. All of us must stay in harmony with the
orchestra of life, even though our instruments may be different. Although
killing fish may be perfectly appropriate for one player, it may not be for
another, so you have to allow your own soul to direct you.

Each should play his own tune and stay within the harmony of his life
and not judge anyone else's playing. In order to be harmonious with God,
you must have balance.

Many of us carry big old backpacks around with us, filled with all the
hurts and heavy burdens that we have clung to throughout our lives. So
when we try to establish harmony, we need to detach from all the pain
that is weighing us down.

When I was a very little girl I remember that I was enthralled with a fel-
low in our neighborhood. I really admired him, and one day I was trying
to impress him. I was climbing trees and performing antics to get his

attention. He turned and looked at me and said, "Don't try to do what all the boys do. You're ugly anyway."

I was so hurt that the memory stayed with me for a long, long time. Because he meant so much to me, he had the ability to rip my heart. You know, some people can say degrading things to you and you can let their comments pass. But when it is someone you admire and whose approval you are seeking, such a remark can be devastating. Many of us still carry scars from our early childhood after we become adults.

You can't reach the top of the mountain if you are weighted down by the burdens you carry on your back. You have to take time to sit and rest and to pull all of the excess weight out of your backpack: the anger, the hurts, the guilt, whatever is weighing you down. You must be able to free yourself from the garbage of the past in order to get in harmony with yourself and with nature so that you can enjoy the climb.

Some of the things in our backpack are feelings we have stuffed in there that could have been released by having a good cry. Often we don't even remember what we've packed in there. We have to look inside to see what we've been carrying. When we've taken a good look at the emotions we've been lugging and realize they are hindering our progress and preventing our happiness, we can let them go. When we've removed all the garbage and released the weight on our shoulders, the upward climb will be so much easier.

We may have to look at each burden as we pull it out of the pack. If we want to have a good cry over it in order to leave it behind, what's wrong with that? Sometimes shedding tears is the best way to turn loose of a heavy weight, especially when it has been submerged for so long we had almost forgotten it was there.

We affect our balance with the Spirit by hiding things that should be confronted and released. It is never too late to release them with tears that should have been shed at the time we pretended we weren't hurt.

I look at the harmony of the earth, and I know that I can always find a confirmation of this truth in nature. When the earth becomes so stressed that she has to find release, we have an earthquake or a volcanic eruption. It is like having a nervous breakdown. It's nothing to be ashamed of. It is a cleansing process, a way of getting rid of all of the things that are causing stress and tension. It is Earth's way of getting back in balance.

We need to do the same. We cannot let our tensions build up within us and stay in harmony with Spirit. We must listen to what the Spirit is telling us and follow the guidance in order to find divine peace.

Take a good look at what is causing discord in your life. If it is a discordant relationship that is tearing you apart, don't think that you have to make the music work. If the tunes you are playing are not in harmony, walk away. Regain your own harmony. Perhaps then you can go back and help the other person get in tune, but if the combined notes are causing a cacophony, don't stay and let your notes become sour. You need to stay in balance or you cannot make music with somebody else.

Suppression is not the answer. Don't let suppressed feelings become a cancer within you. Because pain that is stuffed deep inside of you will erupt in negative effects upon your body. Face the pain. Use whatever means is necessary to release it, but exonerate and liberate yourself.

I looked through my Bible to find out what Jesus had taught regarding harmony. Do you know, I found no reference to the word in his teachings. So I asked the Holy Spirit why there were no lessons about harmony in the Master's teaching. And the Spirit said, He *was* harmony. Wherever he went he demonstrated harmony.

When seeking a place to live we must find an area that is in harmony with our own vibrations in order for us to stay in balance. If we have been working to raise our vibrations to a more spiritual level and we go to a city, or an area of a city where the vibrations are in conflict with ours, we feel totally out of balance. It affects our nervous system, and we can't wait to get back to a place where the vibrations are compatible with ours. When we have found such a place, we know that we are home.

But remember that harmony begins in our own hearts. We cannot find it outside ourselves. Ask the Holy Spirit to guide you. It has to come through Him, not from somebody else. You must create it within yourself so that you can share it with others. Strive to do as the Master Jesus did, *be* the harmony. Fine tune yourself and then make beautiful music in your life.

Power Is Born in
the Silence of Humility

PART SIX

▼

POWER OF THE HEART

Preparing for Your Soul Mate

There is a power surge going on right now. I've heard it referred to by different names; nevertheless, there is a definite change in spiritual and personal power that is taking place throughout the world. I can liken it to what I experienced this week while I was meditating. It was like going from a 110 to a 220 circuit. Literally, there are changes in people's bodies. There are changes in people's minds. Also, there are many passing over to the other side now whom we didn't expect to go. Many people are going through tremendous changes.

This power is a positive thing. If somebody goes home, it is not a negative situation. It can be negative if we try to hold them here, but if we release them, it can be very positive. I've known many who have passed over within the last six months and some who are now in the process. Some transitions have absolutely surprised me. But that is what's happening. The 110 power we have been under is over with, and the 220 is coming in!

At the time they incarnated, some people agreed to stay only until this time, and so they are leaving. Many, many people are leaving now. But it's a time of joy, and it's a time of grounding. Those of us who are staying have to be adjusted in order to adapt to the new frequencies. Every part of us must change. Our eating habits will change. We will change in a physical sense, because our vibrations will be changing.

While I was envisioning this, I kept seeing electrical wires: the positive, the negative, and the grounding wires. We desperately need the grounding wire right now, because as this energy pours in, it sends some of us a bit off the deep end!

Sometimes you can't get centered enough to meditate or to pray, because the energy is so strong you feel as though you are going in twenty different directions. But when a piece of equipment is being rewired, the power has to be disengaged for a while. You can't change the wiring from a 110 to a 220 while it is plugged in, because the wires are being stripped.

Many of you are experiencing situations in your work, in your marriage, or in family relationships where you feel as though your nerves are being stripped raw. It's okay. It's a part of the process.

Some who feel as though their wires are broken are looking for a mate who can fix them. The bitter truth is: you have to work on your own spiritual wiring first. You have to mend the things that are broken inside. You must let the Holy Spirit come in and repair the frayed wires: the hurts, the anger, the losses. Let Him come in with all His love, strip you bare, and work on your wiring. Because two wires joined together, as an extension of each other, to produce light, have to be perfect in order to connect. You can't join a functioning wire with a broken wire and expect a good connection. It won't work.

Those of you who are looking for mates, please remember this important point. The Holy Spirit wants to strip you and remove the areas that are blocked so that you won't go into shock when the power is turned on. Wiring can look fine on the outside, but you can't always see where it's broken. So if you are waiting for someone special to come into your life, know that he or she is probably waiting in the wings. When you have done your rewiring, that person will come, as an extension of you, not to take over your light but to produce more light. That is very important. Be patient and use discretion. You don't need to unite with another whose wiring is broken.

It is hard, and sometimes embarrassing, to be stripped down, to have your wires exposed, and to go through all the distress you have to endure.

Some of you are taking care of people at home who are sick or going through traumas. This may seem like a negative, but actually, the positive comes through the strength that the care of that person brings forth in you. Sometimes it seems extremely trying having to care for someone or just to be around a person who is ill. Yet in doing so, you are taking a negative and making a positive. Service is always a grounding experience, so by being a caretaker, you are completing the whole circuit: the negative, the positive, and the grounding. You are bringing power into your life by serving others.

You are being watched over. You are being cared for, and as the Holy Spirit moves through you at this time, He will give you all the strength that you need and will make you into that complete 220, powerful person.

Sometimes when one is experiencing difficulties, it seems as though the problems are never-ending, especially if you are caring for someone who is ill. You may feel as though it is the same drudgery, day in and day out, with no one there to support you or to help. Or if you are going through a divorce, the pain may seem so incredible, you feel that no one can understand. Yet, you see, situations like this are part of the training to make us into the 220 power line that God is creating all over the earth right now.

In the book of Exodus, we are told about Moses having pleaded to Pharaoh to let the Children of Israel leave their work so they could spend three days in the wilderness to worship their God. Pharaoh became angry and told the taskmasters to withhold the straw that the people were combining with mud to make bricks. Yet he required the same amount of bricks to be made. So the people had to compile bricks using only the mud. This increased the difficulty of their work a hundred fold, and the people became resentful. Yet through these trials, they were being prepared for freedom.

Both physically, because of the extra work, and spiritually, through the challenge of oppression, they were being strengthened for the great trials which lay ahead, which led to their freedom and a better life than they could have imagined.

Now, when we feel we are standing alone and are faced with seemingly impossible situations, we often wonder: *what is The Spirit doing to me? I am trying so hard to do what has to be done to help myself and my family, and I don't understand.* I am sure that the children of Israel did not understand when they had to pound their legs in the mud so much faster in their efforts to make bricks without straw. They must have felt angry and helpless. Yet their legs were becoming stronger and stronger to prepare them for their long walk to freedom. Their far-ranging trek required them to be both physically and spiritually strong.

So if you are emotionally down right now and are feeling powerless and helpless, remember that there is a plan. Your spirit is being made stronger by the adversity. The negative, the positive, and the grounding are necessary for this 220 power to streak across the earth and through each and every one of us..

When two batteries are put together in a flashlight, it is the negative touching the positive that creates light. It's not negative/negative nor positive/positive, it's the two conditions in your life, both positive and negative, that mold you into light.

If the circumstances in your life now seem negative, and you don't understand, look for the positive. Ask yourself, what is being created in me? What strength is being brought forth? How is this situation preparing me to become light?

Think of yourself as a power tool. You have to be plugged in, but you also need to be turned on. I've seen many people who are spiritually plugged in, but they don't always get turned on, spiritually, so their power is being wasted. They need your help. Guide them to see the reflection of the Holy Spirit in themselves. If you can turn them on, their power is incredible!

We are power tools in the Spirit's hands. We can be used at any time, day or night. We are being wired right now. We will be turned on when the time is right, and we must let the hand of the Spirit direct us. Because, when our switch is on, we are powerful!

This power surge is happening everywhere. I was sitting with a friend in Phoenix one day recently. We were conversing and, suddenly, I got a headache across my forehead and the base of my skull. She turned to me and asked, "Are you pulling that power down on your own?" She could actually feel it!

It is happening right now. I know many are dealing with inner turmoil. The change is here. If you haven't yet experienced it, you will. God is bringing this power through at a tremendous rate. It is affecting everyone.

Let yourself be rewired. You can be used like an electric sander or a buffer. When the power flows through you, you can help others smooth all their rough edges. But wait for the power to flow. Don't try to force it. When it is connected, if you are wired properly, it will happen. The old 110 power is being shut down. You are becoming dynamic. Don't be afraid of it. If you start having dreams and visions, do not be frightened by them.

The Christian people call this period the second coming. The New Age believers have various names for it. It doesn't matter what it's called, just know that this power change is coming: 110 to 220. Many will be confused and will seek help. If your light is shining, you will attract them. Those who need to be cleansed will come to you soiled. Don't turn them away. Listen to what the Spirit is saying to you, because you are His power tool.

Be sure that your own wiring is intact before you seek a mate. Ask the Holy Spirit to help you. Allow Him to adjust your wiring, and He will gently splice you and repair the areas that are frayed so that when your mate comes, you will be ready. Your own light will become brighter, and your mate will become an extension of that light so that, united, you will produce a flame that will reach farther out and be more powerful.

Mother/Father God, I thank you for your love that surrounds us day and night. I thank you for your power that is here today, and for the new power evolving here on earth. I know that we are becoming like brilliant floodlights, and so I ask that you would give us your grace and your mercy when other people turn against us because our light is too bright.

When at times we feel the hatred around us and the judgment, let us realize that is not because our light is growing dimmer but that it has become so bright it causes discomfort to those who live in darkness.

Help us not to burn out at this time but to be still for the rewiring. Prepare us to receive this new kind of spiritual energy. Join us together as one, that we may become transmitters of this power on earth and help set others free. Use us as buffers to smooth their rough edges with Your love, that we can help them to shine and to see Your reflection within themselves.

Teach us not to be impatient, upset or angry. For those whose spiritual legs are being tried and whose spiritual hearts are being tested, grant them a greater strength and a knowing, as with the children of Israel, that they are being prepared for freedom and a stronger power.

We thank you for all that you are doing. And so it is.

A Leap of Faith Is
Only One Step Away

PART SEVEN

▼

FAITH OF THE HEART

Using Your Faith in Today's World

Matthew 17:24 says: *After Jesus and his disciples arrived in Capernaum, the collectors of the half-shekel tax went up to Peter and said, "Does not your teacher pay the tax?" He said, "Yes." And when he came home, Jesus spoke to him first, saying, "What do you think, Simon? From whom do kings of the earth take toll or tribute? From their sons or from others?" And when he said, "From others," Jesus said to him, "Then the sons are free. However, not to give offense to them, go to the sea and cast a hook, and take the first fish that comes up, and when you open its mouth you will find a shekel; take that and give it to them for me and for yourself."*

Wouldn't you like to pay your tax like that? You know, when the bill comes you just go fishing and reel in the amount due! But in my life, and I'm sure in your's, strong faith is demanded of you before the finances come so easily.

-63-

Think about Peter. He was a commercial fisherman who fished with nets, collecting hundreds of fish at one time. Jesus, being a master, could have manifested the money right there and then. But no. He sends Peter out to go fishing with a rod and tells him the first fish he catches will have the needed money in its mouth. Talk about a tall fish story!

Even though Peter had spent much time with the master Jesus, don't you think he must have wondered, is the Master pulling my leg, or what? He knew that Jesus could have manifested the money immediately as easily as putting it in the mouth of a fish. Following those instructions must have taken a great deal of trust. You wonder how long Peter was down by the sea wrestling with his faith before he caught that fish.

I have this problem with faith all the time. Instead of my having to follow instructions, I wonder why the Holy Spirit doesn't just give me what I need? But if He did, I wouldn't have to stretch and grow, and I wouldn't learn what I need to learn. God seems to take his time with us, and so he always sends us fishing. The fishing trip may seem bizarre, but by the testing of our faith, we learn and we grow.

If you are having problems with your finances, and you, like Peter, are being asked to step out in faith first, you are going to have to do it. That is how you move forward, for when you are doing the work of the Spirit, you are always being tested

Remember the story of Jesus and the loaves and fishes? Well, if I were in a crowd of people who were extremely hungry and I had a couple of jelly doughnuts, I would be afraid to tell folks to sit down and prepare to eat. I think I first would ask the Holy Spirit to multiply the jelly doughnuts so that there would be enough for everybody.

The Master Jesus didn't need to do this, because he understood universal law and could manifest things in the blink of an eye. He simply said, "Father, thank you for these fishes and these loaves." He broke the bread and gave it and the fish to his disciples, telling them to serve all the people. They did, and there were twelve basketfuls of food left over!

This was a demonstration of faith to the people. Why is it that we lack the faith that Jesus had? Why are we always wanting things and needing things? It doesn't matter whether we are big business executives or simple homemakers, all of us have the same needs. The only difference is that wealthy business men have more and higher bills, but they need the same amount of faith as the ones who have only household expenses to pay. The big executive, too, needs to depend on the Holy Spirit for his help.

Now, if you are going to manifest bread, make sure it is fresh. Stale bread is hard to get down. You need the oil of the Spirit to soften it. Get it fresh daily from the Holy Spirit. Don't choose a place where stale bread is served because you lack the faith to manifest anything better. God has given you the basket and the ability to fill it yourself in order to satisfy your needs.

So if your faith provides a place which serves you fresh spiritual bread and fish, go there and receive all you can. Don't settle for anything less because you lack faith or feel unworthy of receiving better. Go to the ovens of the Holy Spirit and receive spiritual food that is warm and fresh, for that will build your faith and keep it strong.

Recently, It seemed as though everything in my life had been going wrong. I was feeling insecure in my spiritual work. I had spoken before a group and felt that my talk had bombed. The state of my finances were worrying me. Our two fourteen-year-old dogs had died, and I was not only feeling the loss but was concerned about the vet bills the dogs had incurred.

I considered giving up my fifteen-year mission of spiritual teaching so I could get a job. During my meditation that day I sat for an hour and cried. I asked God, would you do just this for me: give me confirmation that the last message I presented touched someone who heard it, and— just to let me know that I've been doing the right thing—would you send me some financial aid, no matter how small.

After a while I went upstairs and found there was a message on the answering machine. A precious person had called and said, "I just wanted to tell you that the message you brought a couple of weeks ago really helped me in my life." I shed tears of joy, because this was exactly what I had asked for. The Holy Spirit had answered my prayer. I don't know if that person knew that he was led by the Spirit. The next day I received a note from him, thanking me again, and there was money with it! I knew without a shadow of a doubt that the Holy Spirit had spoken to me: *Move out in faith, and I'll provide for you.*

This person had lifted me up and boosted my faltering faith when I was floundering and didn't know what to do. So if ever the Holy Spirit calls upon you to do something, even if it's small—such as making a phone call to encourage someone—whatever it is, do it. Because you might be preventing another from giving up.

Many times in my life I've wished that when the Lord assigned me a task He would *first* provide the means. Because it is so humiliating to fail when challenged to step out in faith. And so I caution you, when you follow your spiritual guidance, be sure that the assignment came from the Spirit. Examine it with your heart, be convinced of its source, and know that you are doing it for the right reasons. Make sure that there is no pride involved or intent of financial gain, but that your goals are spiritual. When you are satisfied that this is the case, you can step out with confidence, for you won't be able to go in any other direction.

When I came to Payson eleven years ago, it was a tiny little mountain town. Someone said to me, "Why don't you start a group here like you had in Phoenix?" I said, "Oh no, I don't think so!" I was really worn out from that previous venture. A year had passed, but I still felt burned out. Yet the suggestion made was being confirmed over and over again. You know, once God puts the seed in your heart, you get confirmation everywhere you turn. You may not get the means, but you get the confirmation.

Finally I agreed to do it. But I said to the Holy Spirit, "Please, may I have a job, just till Christmas, and I'll continue to do all the work for you that I've been doing." Then I walked into a little Christian bookstore to get some Christmas presents for my children, and the lady said, "Oh,

Vanda, I'm so glad you came in today. Would you like a job?" I said, "Oh, I would love to have a job!" Then she said, "I can't pay you anything, but we can trade." Then I realized that I should have been more specific in my request!

But I knew the Lord was speaking to my heart. I worked at the bookstore for a year and a half and met every pastor in town, so I was asked to speak at every church. It was incredible the opportunities the Spirit set up for me there. I was asked to initiate a little spiritual group. So I arranged with the school system to rent a small room in one of the schools. The rent wasn't too expensive, so we started our group called "Living Waters—Saturday Night Praise."

I told myself that I was going to walk out in faith, because I didn't know where the money was to come from, but I felt that we needed to get things started. We had fliers prepared, and we were busy getting everything set up when the lady from the school called and asked, "Vanda, do you have insurance?" And I asked, "Why do I need insurance?" She said, "Well, you're a nondenominational group aren't you? If you are to meet at the school, you will need half a million dollars' worth of insurance."

Oh my! I knew there must be a catch to this somewhere; everything was just too easy. I went into one of those complaining modes. I felt like such a fool. We had put out all these fliers and were ready to go and then found we needed insurance we couldn't afford!

Now sometimes when the challenge looks overwhelming, you're afraid to take another step. But when I did call the local insurance company and told them how much liability insurance I needed, the lady said, "Well, that's not so bad." She said it would be $500 a quarter, or something like that. It may as well have been the moon! We didn't have it. Yet I told her that I guessed we would have it but I wasn't sure when. She said, "If you are to start on Saturday, you will have to have it in by then. I said okay.

I told a few people involved the amount we would have to raise, and we all stepped out in faith.

First, a lady took part of her social security check to the insurance company and told them, "This is for the Living Water Saturday Night Praise Group. The agent asked her name, but the lady declined to give it. She said that she wasn't a part of the group but had heard of it and wanted to contribute.

Little by little, people came into the bookstore and made donations toward the project. Someone had a garage sale and brought in the money she had made. So the finances came forward. But, you see, first I had to cast the line. That is what you have to do in any situation involving faith.

I promise you that if your mission is from God, the means will come. People will help, and the plan will work. Just examine yourself and ask, is there any pride or ego prompting my efforts in this endeavor? If your only reason is to serve the Holy Spirit, the goal will be reached. It is time to go fishing!

Remember that Jesus didn't hesitate to have the people sit down and prepare to eat. His faith in the Spirit was unquestioning. So if you lack anything that seemingly prevents you from accomplishing your mission, surrender to the Spirit, put your total trust in His ability to provide, and whatever you need will come. I've seen it happen over and over and over again.

When you are faced with a block that seems like a wall between you and your goal, just remember old Peter standing by the sea and casting his line into the water.

One Thanksgiving, in Phoenix, we had invited sixty or more people to come for dinner. I didn't know where the food was coming from. I just knew that those people were supposed to be there, because they were alone and needy. The Holy Spirit told me to go out and buy three turkey roasters. Being of little faith, I went out and bought two. I put them on the counter and went to church, feeling really low.

I left the windows down in my old Mustang (I always hoped someone would steal it!), and when we came out of the church, one of my daughters said, "Mom, there's a turkey in the back seat!" We were so excited! So we went home and put that one turkey in the pan. Then a friend brought over a second turkey, and we put that one in the other pan.

I waited and waited for another turkey until it was almost Thanksgiving Day. I asked, where is the third turkey coming from? And I heard the words of the Holy Spirit, clear as day, say to me, "There's no third pan. What do you think you are going to put it in?" Immediately, my heart felt heavy. I realized that my faith had been only strong enough to provide for two turkeys when I had been told to buy three roasters. So I went out and bought a third pan.

At almost the last minute, a man came to me and said that he was going home for Thanksgiving but had been given a fresh turkey which he wanted to give to me. I didn't even have to defrost it! There wouldn't have been time to do so anyway.

So whatever it is you are needing, whether it's a fish with a gold coin in its mouth or extra loaves of bread to feed those already sitting at the table, believe that God adores each and every one of you and is ready to provide. If you'll only remember that you must step out in faith first, it will happen.

ONENESS CAN NOT BE DIVIDED

PART EIGHT

▼

ONENESS OF THE HEART

Finding Direction for Your Life

I have been told that my method of teaching is not traditional. Jesus always taught with parables and talked about lost coins or little kernels of wheat and things of that sort. Today, since we use instant bread mix and have credit cards in our pockets, it's a little hard to relate to things like lost coins or to yeast that raises the bread. So when I meditate and pray, I ask to be given a modern-day parable to share, so that people can understand the message God is sending through me.

During my daily meditations, I ask to see into the hearts of the people I am to teach and to be given the right message for them. This week I received the words *spiritual food*. As the week went on, I grew frustrated because I hadn't received the whole gist of the message. One day I was in the kitchen baking cakes, and the Spirit came to me and said, "This is the message." And I thought, what? Cake? I am to take them a message about a *cake?*

By the end of the week I was feeling really insecure. I prayed, "Well, God, I'll do whatever you want me to do, but please confirm the message about the cake. The day went by, and the message wasn't confirmed, but I was starting to receive little bits here and there. Then a lady from the group where I was to speak called and said, "It's the birthday of our group tomorrow and we wondered if you could stay for some cake." I knew this was the confirmation I had been asking for. It is always very important for me to have my subject confirmed. So we are going to talk about a spiritual cake, but first let's reflect a bit on our daily bread.

In the Lord's prayer, Jesus taught us to say, "Give us this day our daily bread." He didn't say give us day-old bread, or give us this day some stale bread, or enough bread for a week, He said give us our daily bread. That means it is fresh. It's fresh from the oven of the Holy Spirit. It's something you receive on a daily basis, something you have to go to God for, not once in a great while, but daily. Meditation and prayer must be a daily process.

This concept is challenging for us, because we are all taught we must provide for ourselves and have enough food for the week. It's the same with spiritual food. Some of us are holding down two or three jobs, with both moms and dads working, so it's difficult to go to God every day for daily bread. But we must. You know that if you eat bread that's old, it seems to stick in your throat. Some teachings ram old bread down your throat with no water of the Spirit to wash it down, and it's so stale that it's hard to swallow. Yet every day we can go to God for fresh bread.

It is difficult for young people, too, to find time to ask God for what they need. They are so busy with their school activities they feel there is no time for anything else. Yet it is necessary for them to have, each day, their daily bread. Jesus told us how to pray, and it is important to ask for what we need. It's all right to go to God every day and say I'm hungry. We don't need to go to anyone else for the spiritual food and guidance we need. Just accept that fresh, puffy, hot-from-the-oven bread of the Holy Spirit.

Now let me show you how to make a spiritual cake.

First we need a timer. God's timing usually seems way too slow for us. When you are struggling with a lot of difficulties, the timer seems to tick on forever. Yet no matter what you are going through, know that God's timing is perfect. Whether in the work place, school, home, or wherever you are, God is bringing into your life the right ingredients to mix together and create a perfect spiritual cake.

Now, most of us don't like to mix too much with other people. We like to be alone a little bit. You see, to be constantly mixed with other people can be challenging, but God's ultimate goal for us all is oneness! Oneness is what results when different ingredients are blended together. And so the blending of diverse personalities produces a spiritual oneness.

So the timer is set and is running. I am always trying to hurry God up, aren't you? Sometimes I actually wait patiently, but not very often. I'm usually trying to push Him along. *Hasn't that five minutes gone by, yet? Hasn't that ten minutes passed? It's been a year, Lord, and I'm still suffering, and I need you.* He never varies His scheduled timing.

The next thing we need for our spiritual cake is the bowl. It is where the mixing takes place: at work, home, school, wherever you are. This is where we all get blended together. I dislike it at times. Sometimes God will put us in a glass bowl where everyone can see whatever is happening to us. It may seem degrading to us to be so exposed, but He will use whatever bowl is necessary for unfolding our spiritual perfection.

Then we have the beater. This is used when we haven't blended together well. God then uses his hand to stir things up for us. For example, He may bring about conditions which force us to change jobs, or to have a lifestyle change for other reasons, such as divorce or illness. Whatever the circumstances, welcome them as part of the blending process.

Now for the ingredients. God always gives us just the right amounts of everything: the right amount of trouble, the right amount of financial problems, or marital problems, whatever it takes to help us grow and to come into the universal oneness.

First there's the flour. We all know the process of the flour. When wheat first appears, it is green. It's head stands high, because when you're green you always have your head in the air and are kind of snooty! But as the wheat begins to grow, the weight of the kernels makes the stalk bow. It's the bowed head that is wise. It's the bowed head that is full of grain. It's the lowered head that God is ready to harvest.

It may take many painful situations to get to that place. You've been fertilized. The manure in your life wasn't so great. But you've grown, and a lot of you have reached the place now where, having been humbled, God can literally harvest you. You all know that in the harvesting process, the bent head is cut from the stem. Then it's thrashed. Many of us are in the thrashing process now, and we don't feel very well, because it is so difficult.

Yet you reach the place where you are like the flour in this cake. You think that you've been through so much that you've been ground into almost nothing. Some don't like the flour people very well, because they are sort of plain and washed out and dry. Just remember that whoever those people are in your life, they've gone through a very hard process.

After you get to this point, you think that God must be through with you, that you have suffered enough, but He takes the sieve and He sifts you, as if it weren't enough that you've endured all the grinding. You think you can't possibly take any more, but God finds that there are lumps in your life. He wants them out. Because, He can't blend people together smoothly if one of them is lumpy. Whether caused by anger, hatred, or other negative conditions, those lumps can't stay. Lumpy flour cannot blend smoothly into the oneness of the cake.

So if God is sifting you right now, and you are having a hard time, remember, He has to remove the lumps—it is His love that does it—because He is bringing us all into the oneness.

Then we have the sugar. If there are some people in your life who seem to you to be sickeningly sweet and boring, remember that it took a lot for them to get into this position. They, too, went through the thrashing. They, too, went through the cutting down, the humiliation of being severed from the stalk. They went through the drying out. So if someone comes bouncing into your life who seems sickeningly sweet, don't judge him or her too quickly. Because the saccharin individuals, too, have been ground and sifted.

Next we have the salt. I have known some people who seemed a little salty. Sometimes we refer to gentlemen who are a bit crude as being salty! But, you see, they reveal the religiosity in us. They can help us to grow. We may need to be conservative in allowing them in our lives, but we do require a little pinch to make all the other flavors come out.

So if such a person comes along and you feel he isn't as spiritual as you and consider him crude, remember that God sent him along for a reason. Whether it's Jack or Joe, or whoever, if you can't learn the required lesson from him, there will be another Jack or Joe just around the corner. So allow the salt, just a little.

When all the ingredients are in the bowl God stirs the mixture together. It's not that the sugar particularly wants to blend with the flour, or the flour with the salt, but in order to come into the oneness, this is what has to happen. So if in your school or workplace you are seated beside someone you don't really like very much, remember to try to love that person. Otherwise, others like him are going to take his place. He is a part of your cake, and you need to be mixed together.

Now we come to the egg people. These are the people who are quite self-sufficient, self-contained! They are in their own little shell, and they don't want to mix with others, because they consider themselves spiritually perfect. However, when you have that attitude, God enters in and literally smashes you open to show you that you were being perfected so that you could be blended into His beautiful spiritual cake.

Some of us are at the stage where we have reached our idea of perfection, and we don't want to be broken. We've worked hard to get where we are, and we don't want to mix in with those who have gone a different direction. But that is not God's intention for us.

There's one ingredient we haven't yet put into our cake. It's the one which I am especially fond of: the nuts. Perhaps I feel it best characterizes me. If you are a nut because people have driven you nuts, or because you were a little nutty anyway, you are very much needed in every spiritual cake, in every church or group, in every family. "A merry heart doeth good like a medicine." When life seems really depressing, there's nothing like someone who can bring a little merriment into it.

So I like the nuts a lot. You know, even though they blend into the cake, they always keep their singleness, their individuality. I like to think they are like the leaders. They have to be cracked open. They have to go through a process, but they do blend in.

At this point the batter is a little stiff. The reason we are a little stiff when we come together—the flour people, the salty people, the sweet people, the very spiritual people—is that we haven't added shortening. Without the oil of the Holy Spirit, we are dry. We can't make a cake without oil. It doesn't matter how well we've been perfected nor how much breaking we've been through, if we haven't been blended with the oil of the Holy Spirit we are not complete. We'll never rise to complete our mission in life.. We'll never be able to be put into the baptism of fire, because we wouldn't come out whole.

So it is the oil of the Holy Spirit that we need to pray for, as groups, as churches, as schools, or in our marriages and families. When things get kind of rocky, pray for the oil of the Holy Spirit. That's what makes the cake light and fluffy and holds everything together. God's love is like oil. It mixes and holds us together. In the Bible, The Holy Spirit is referred to as oil, and also as living water.

So with the blending of these ingredients we finally have a cake. We have a oneness of all the broken people who have been through all the processes, as teenagers, as moms, as fathers, as leaders. If we'll allow ourselves to be blended into this oneness, in accordance with God's plan, then we can all go into the fire.

Now, why do you need to be put into an oven after you've gone through all of this mixing? Jesus talks about a baptism of fire. Some have experienced it, some haven't. It's a very real process, and sometimes you feel as though God has deserted you, because the heat is so intense. You may be in a group but feel like a separate part of it, because you feel so frightened. Some of you are going through the fire right now. Whether it involves finances, or health, or other trials, God has his hand on you. But He does have the oven on.

You are not going to become that spiritual cake unless you go into the oven. The timer is set according to God's timing. If the cake is taken out before the set time, it is going to be doughy in the middle. We don't need doughy middles! We need to be baked until we are light and high so that we can be spiritual food for others. We weren't put here to experience only joy. We must go through the whole process, all the trying circumstances we've had to endure.

We are all in different stages of this process. If you are coming out of the procedure, hold your hand out to those who are just going in. Be the spiritual food for others.

Don't give up. Don't be fearful because God has given you just enough bread for today. Remember the children of Israel when they were given the manna? One day's worth was all they could have. If they were given more, it would perish.

They must have thought: God, we had such a rough time in Egypt, why can't we have bread for a couple of day's, at least, so we won't have to beseech you so often? But, you see, He sees every heart, and He wants every heart dependent upon Him. When you trust in Him, you don't get hurt so badly. In fact, it becomes kind of fun, trusting in Him every day.

We would like to provide for ourselves. We want better jobs with more money so we won't have to depend on God so much. We tell God we will tithe and worship Him, but we want to take care of ourselves. But God wants us to lean on Him day after day after day.

If you're in school and other students are giving you a bad time, God sees that, but He's only going to give you enough grace for today. He won't promise to make everything all right for the next week or two unless you ask for His grace each day. Ask for daily bread. That's what we require.

After the cake comes out of the oven, there is a cooling period. A time when you can finally be still and just cool off. Most of you haven't experienced that part of the process yet, but I promise you it is coming, a time when you can literally be still, stop the struggle, and cool off. Then you truly become spiritual food for many. Your traumas are preparing you to help others. The tears are a part of the cooling-down process, so it's okay to let them flow.

It is only after complete processing that you will begin to see clearly your direction for life! If you will reach out to each other, I promise you that, together, we will become a most wonderful spiritual cake!

FEAR KEEPS CHASING UNTIL YOU STOP RUNNING FROM IT

▼

PART NINE

A GIVING HEART

Holding On Past the Deadline

One day this week, as I sat in meditation, I was told: "You can't put all your eggs in one basket." Instead of sharing our spiritual wisdom and other assets, such as our money or our time, we tend to keep them all inside ourselves in our spiritual basket. We keep our spiritual gifts inside, because we are afraid to let them out. So, in essence, we are putting all our eggs in one basket. If our basket is already full we have no room to add new spiritual gifts that we receive.

As I considered this and thought about the egg, I noted that an egg has a hard shell on the outside but the food inside is soft. The soft part of the egg represents spiritual food. Some of us, because of painful experiences, tend to have a hard shell at times. Now, if the shell is so hard that it can't be broken, we are not going to be able to give our spiritual food to others.

When people are chosen for service by the Spirit, they are often broken. It is the breaking that allows the softness to come forth. If you are not broken several times in your life, it is not likely that you are going to be able to give your spiritual gifts.

Now, if you are a healer or a teacher, or whatever your spiritual focus is, others tend to offend you. They don't always understand the challenges you go through and the many sacrifices you have to make. To protect yourself, you develop a hard shell. In order for your softness to feed another's spiritual hunger, you have to let the Spirit break your shell. Let Him crack your protective armor and release your spiritual food.

If a chicken kept her eggs inside, she could not provide food for us. If we keep our treasures hidden inside, how can we provide spiritual food for others? The eggs in our spiritual baskets are meant to be distributed.

Some of you have been called to speak or to serve and you're afraid to follow the calling, perhaps because you have so often been hurt. But the eggs, or spiritual food, within you will spoil if left too long in your basket. Those gifts inside of you can atrophy if you fail to use them.

Often it is fear which prevents us from using the gifts that we have been given. We refuse to discuss with others what is in our hearts for fear of their reactions. We are afraid of getting egg in our face! Usually the response we fear is not the response we receive at all. We must let go of our fears and put our trust in the Holy Spirit.

How do we replace fear with faith? Through wisdom. How do we acquire wisdom? Through experience. By facing the things that we fear. By looking at the challenge, examining it, and asking ourselves: why am I afraid of this? Fear can put so many obstacles in our lives, we must learn to surrender it, to turn the fearful situation over to the Holy Spirit, and allow Him to handle it.

Some time ago, when I was living in Beaver Valley, a friend and her teenage son came to visit me. She said, "Don't worry about dinner, we've already eaten." I thought, that's good, because I don't have anything to serve. We visited a while and then went to bed. The next morning when I awakened, I thought, "Oh, God! I don't have anything to give them for breakfast." And the Holy Spirit said very clearly to me, "Take them out to breakfast." And I thought, "What? Do you think I won the lottery or something? How can I do this?"

Spirit reminded me that I had 80 dollars in my account toward my Arizona Public Service bill, which was short of the 95 dollars I owed. Nevertheless, I was again told to take my friends out to breakfast. So I took out 20 dollars, and we went to a cafe and ordered their all-you-can-eat special. We sat there and ate all the things that we normally considered bad for us, while laughing and talking as we watched my friend's big, strapping son put away piles of food.

We were having a great time, but I kept thinking about that APS bill. I had received a notice that they were going to disconnect my electricity the next day. (When you get bills in the mail that are a different color from their regular bills, you know you're in trouble!) Well, I was terribly afraid that they were going to turn off my electricity. But the Holy Spirit told me that He would replace that 20 dollars.

Still I worried about it all day long. Finally Spirit asked me, "What are you afraid of?" I said, "Well, you know, I'm afraid they are going to turn off my electricity." But the Spirit repeated, "What are you afraid of?"

Well, I thought about it and realized that I had a wood-burning stove to keep me warm and on which I could cook. I had candles for light. And I wondered, what *am* I afraid of? So I faced the fear head-on and realized how foolish it was to be so afraid just because my electricity might be disconnected. That was when I felt a tremendous release, because I let go of that ridiculous fear. But I had to look at it before I recognized that I had no reason to be so frightened. When I did, it was as though a big weight had been lifted off me. I thought, well, nobody but the APS people are going to know about it anyway.

That evening a man who lived across the street came over. I had taken him a bowl of lentil soup earlier, because I felt I should take him something. He thanked me and told me he was quite tired and just wanted to kick back and get some sleep. About half an hour later I saw him driving down the hill toward town. I thought that was strange. Pretty soon he came back and knocked on my door. He handed me a carton of toffee-brickle ice cream, which is my absolute favorite. I took it and decided to have a bowl. When I opened the carton, there was a hundred dollar bill on top!

That's how God works! But you have to let go of your fear. You can't hold onto it. It lowers your vibrations. It's hard to receive when you're in a state of fear.

The next thought I had during meditation was about receiving a mate. Many of you have been promised a mate and are trying hard to find him or her. Some of you feel you are getting too old for this. I would remind you of the Christmas story. Mary probably thought she was too young to be pregnant with the promise! Then there was Elizabeth who no doubt thought she was too old to be pregnant with the promise. Yet both of them bore children.

Your promise is coming. Your physical age has nothing to do with what God is bringing to you. You must relinquish the doubts, though. It is not productive to keep running around to all the places where you think you might meet that special person. If you're looking for someone intelligent, you can't keep haunting the library, hoping to find someone there. Whatever characteristics you are looking for, don't keep going to the places where you think that type of person might go. Give your desire to the Holy Spirit and trust in Him.

You have to let your promise go. You can't keep holding onto it so tightly that it can't fly. You're not going to meet your mate exactly the way you think you are. The person you were promised is out there and is coming, but you have to let that person come to you. It's like flying a kite. If you want it to fly high, you have to let go of it. You can hold onto a little string of faith, but you have to give your desire to the Holy Spirit. He knows what He's doing. so don't allow yourself to be an obstruction.

My husband David was born in the United States, and I was born in England. Yet where did the Holy Spirit bring us together? In the little town of Payson, Arizona! So don't lose hope. Don't give up. That love is there for you. Let your promise fly, like a balloon. Let it be lifted by the Spirit. Let the wind of the Spirit blow you where you need to go, and you will meet the person you are supposed to meet. It might happen in the location you are in, or it may be in another state or country, but that love will come.

Please remember Mary and Elizabeth—too old, too young? No. The pregnancy of promise is upon everyone the Holy Spirit has spoken to. Don't put up restrictions and decide that your mate has to look a certain way or be a specific type. Just know that he or she is out there for you, so you mustn't give up.

Next is the money situation. Money problems can be burdensome, and it takes a lot of patience to be able to keep your faith. But as with everything else, you must free yourself of the limitation of fear in order to receive. Every provision you need will come to you if you follow the directions of the Spirit. Sometimes that's very difficult, because what you are directed to do may not provide very much money. But if you are reaching out to help others and are following your inner guidance, eventually your needs will be met.

When I first moved to Beaver Valley, my rent was $500 a month, and there was no money coming in whatsoever. The man who owned my house lived just across the stream from me. I passed him every day when I walked to the mailbox. He was a dear man, but even though I thought he was a wonderful guy, he didn't appear to me to be in touch with the Spirit.

I longed to stay with the work I was doing, but after the first three months, I owed $1500 that I couldn't pay. I continued teaching, and the Spirit kept telling me, "You must go forward. You cannot do anything else but this." And I thought, *so why are you embarrassing me like this?*

For six months I was unable to pay the rent. I owed this man $3,000! Every time I passed him on the street, I ducked! Can you imagine his seeing me drive by every day with no head? I was just so embarrassed!

When the six months had passed, I sat on my bed and told myself, I just can't do this any more. I had tried to get other jobs, but each time I applied they would tell me I was over qualified. I just couldn't get it together. I had continued teaching, traveling and doing all that I could; but at the end of the six months, I lost my faith and was in tears.

My birthday had just passed when a wealthy lady in Phoenix called and asked, "Can you come down and visit with me for a couple of days? I need some cheering up." I thought, *Gee, I'm not the person to do this!* Nevertheless, I drove down to Phoenix and spent a couple of days with her. We talked about many things. She told me about her birthday, and asked me when mine was. I admitted it was two days ago. She said, "Oh really? I didn't know that."

When I was getting ready to leave, she handed me an envelope. She said, "This is the figure I got for you, and I want you to have it as a birthday present." I thanked her and left. As I was driving up the mountain, I opened it and found $300 in it. I felt very grateful but wasn't sure what I was supposed to do with it. I was too embarrassed to give it to my landlord, because I owed him so much. I thought perhaps I was to use it for a Thanksgiving dinner for those in need.

That night I put it on my dresser. I thanked God for it and asked Him to bless and multiply it and to let me know what the money was for. Then I got into bed, pulled the covers up over me, and sobbed for hours, because I didn't know how I could go on.

At about 11:30 the phone rang. I thought, oh no! Something must have happened to one of my children. But when I answered it, it was the lady I had been staying with. She told me, "Vanda, you know I was just wakened from a dead sleep, and in my dream I realized that I had missed something on the check. Could you please send it back to me." My heart sank, but I told her, "Oh yes, of course." Then she told me, "I'm going to rewrite the check because the zeros are wrong." She sent me a check for $3,000! To the penny. I kid you not!

I can't tell you how happy I was to see the owner of my house the next day. I just jumped out of the car and handed him the money in cash. I told him I was so sorry it had taken me so long. He said, "I knew you would come up with it." He had more faith than I did, I think.

So whatever it is that is frightening you when you are trying to do the work of the Spirit, keep up the work. Don't give up. Whether you are a teacher, a group leader, or are sharing your insights in classes—whatever your service is—know that your needs will be met, Sometimes the Spirit may be a little late in providing your rent in order to teach you faith or patience so that you can stand up before a group and encourage them. If you want to help other people, you have to be able to identify with their problems.

Whatever your challenge may be, you have to release the fear, because fear can set up a block and keep you from connecting with Spirit. Don't be embarrassed if He passes by what you consider to be your deadline. Just know that everything is done in God's perfect timing.

WISDOM IS BORN
BECAUSE OF IGNORANCE

PART TEN

▼

A CHRISTMAS HEART

Allowing

Let us take a look at our beliefs. We all get stuck, at times, in our belief systems. It really doesn't matter what our beliefs are. It only matters that we give each other the freedom to believe. Because in doing that, we blend together and each person becomes part of the big picture. For example, in a jigsaw puzzle, if every piece were the same color and the same shape they could not be made into a completed picture.

Like pieces of a puzzle, we are different colors and various shapes and sizes. It is because of our differences that, when united, we form a cohesive and balanced whole. Together we produce a beautiful, creative and dynamic picture. In the acceptance of our diversity, we find the gratification of our oneness.

This acceptance is necessary in one's spiritual growth. You can take the faster road by going directly into your own heart and by listening to the Holy Spirit, or you can take a more structured path by following any of the theological teachings. It doesn't really matter. All the paths lead to God. All paths lead us Home!

So if somebody criticizes you—and often people who are emerged in only a particular theology tend to be judgmental—it is only because they are infants in their spiritual awareness. So if you are censured because of your freedom of thinking, handle the criticizer as you would a small child. If a baby falls or creates disorder, you don't chastise it, you encourage it to try again.

That's the attitude we need to assume toward those who are still in that childlike state in the spirit, who criticize the way we believe, the way we worship, or the way we feel. Allow them to be children. Allow them to take their own spiritual path, even though it may seem to us to be a tedious one.

Our physicists tell us that everything in the universe is vibrating, each at its own unique rate. This, of course, applies to people. When we increase our awareness and become more spiritual, our rate of vibration automatically rises. If it rises too quickly, we can have a heart attack. It needs to rise slowly. So we must allow others to grow at their own rate.

Therefore, if people have been condemning you because of your beliefs, forgive them, because they are in a place of ignorance. Wisdom actually evolves from ignorance. Ponder this: Our ignorant mistakes cause us to grow.

Yes, wisdom does come from ignorance, and we have all been climbing out of a place of ignorance for many lifetimes. All of us, at one time, have been unenlightened and judgmental. We are still climbing, but what we have become is the result of what God has created in us day by day.

God's Gifts

Next, I would like to talk about the gifts that God has given to us so that we can present our treasures to Him in return. He has given us gifts which help us to become tolerant and allowing toward others.

The Pearl of Wisdom

The Pearl of Wisdom is made from the irritants of life. As we suffer the irritations resulting from our own ignorance, we are growing. It is a learning process. When we try to detach from the irritants, to push them away, the pearl within us fails to grow. We need to allow God to give us the lessons and must accept the irritants, no matter much as we dislike them, so that the pearl can continue to develop within us.

When I was looking at an old oyster shell the other day, I was reminded of how unappealing they are on the outside—rather bumpy, and sandy, not attractive at all. But, it is what is going on inside, because of the irritants, that is so tremendously beautiful.

I have seen so many people who, through all the tests and trials, are producing a spiritual pearl within themselves only to have others take the knife of judgment and, figuratively, cut the oyster open before the pearl is fully developed.

Many of you, I'm sure, have seen this happen. People take the knife of judgment toward someone and start cutting right to the heart, and it retards that person's growth. It causes some people—especially if they're young in spirit—to say, "I don't really love God so much any more because I've been hurt by all the criticism and hate directed toward me. Why did God allow this to happen?" Those individuals might go off by themselves and stop making their pearls, because of the misplaced judgment. We all must stop using the knife of judgment.

Let us forgive those who judge us, because they are children, spiritually. We cannot blame God for their opinions, and if we use their condemnation for our growth, we can be thankful that it occurred. Let's not instead, turn around and stab others and cause them to quit making their pearls. If permitted to continue their growth, those pearls could grow to be gorgeous and become of much greater value.

Let the irritants be a formative catalyst within each person. If an individual is blowing angry bubbles and is not very nice to be around, perhaps unattractive on the outside, leave him alone, because a pearl of great price is being made within.

If you have the chance, pick up an oyster shell and touch the pearl. Touching one, feeling it's smoothness, says something to me. It's telling me, "Let's not hurt one another. Let's allow the people who are growing inside to develop in their own way."

Often I have advised my children, don't do this or don't do that because you might get hurt; but when I was a child, I never learned that way, did you? I thought, oh adults, they don't know anything. I had to take the falls myself, to let my own irritants do the work within me to produce the pearl of wisdom. The experience is a present that God gives to us. We have to embrace the trials so that we can produce gifts for Him in return.

When I am considering God's gifts to us, I think about the gifts those wonderful wise men, or astrologers, presented to the Christ Child. Let us take a look at those gifts.

Gold

First of all, let's consider the gold. We all know the process of mining gold. It is placed into the fire. It is refined through various procedures to become the polished gold that we treasure. How many of you feel that you are sick and tired of the process of being made into pure gold? It seems tedious and never-ending.

I've been shoved into the fire so many times it seems unreal. Then I'm brought out, figuratively pounded, and put back in again. I don't enjoy this at all! When I was a very small child, I recall being told by the Spirit, "If you can survive this abuse, I will make you into gold and you will become a holder of light." And so I see myself as a candlestick—not always shiny gold, but still a holder of light!

When I was growing up, I realized that there was a tremendous amount of abuse, poverty, and degradation in my life. I had parents who told me on a daily basis that they wished I hadn't been born. My father raped me continually, from the time I was very young, and my mother used me for a human punching bag. At that time it seemed to me that God didn't care about me at all, but one day I heard His voice: "I will come into that dark place where you are, and I will mine you out of there and liberate you so you may become a light to help others, if you will only persevere while I chip away the dirt.

Many of you have come from such places and situations, those caves of darkness, and God has touched you and said, "I don't care where you are, whether you're in despair, or have been abused or hurt, I love you, and I'm going to come into that dark cave where you reside. For you are gold, and I am going to burnish you, and wash the dirt from you, and you will become beautiful! However, you must first be put in the spiritual fire a few times, but I will make you into a holder for light." And that's what we all will become, a holder for the Light.

Some of you are still waiting for your mates. Consider this: candlesticks come in pairs. Some are smaller than others. (I like to think of these as the females.) When life seems so cruel that you can no longer handle it alone, and if you've gone through the processing and are ready, have faith that your mate will come and will ignite your fire.

Many of you are fortunate enough to be with the right person now. Others are awaiting that special individual. If you are waiting, don't settle for anyone other than your complimentary mate, because the union won't be harmonious. The Holy Spirit can make you a matching pair. If you will be patient and let your light shine, the right person will come. It's a promise. We all have a soulmate somewhere, and it will happen for you. Just hold on. Keep shining.

We are that gift of gold to God. He molds us with His alchemy, and when we have been transformed into gold, we return it to Him !

Frankincense

The next gift I want to discuss is Frankincense. This gift was taken from a big, hard tree, and the only way to extract frankincense is to pierce the tree to the heart. Out of this comes a resin called *tears*. I kid you not;

it's called tears, the resin tears of frankincense. The only way it can be extracted is to take the knife to the heart, tear it, and let the tears come forth from the tree.

The Holy Spirit uses the same technique on us. The tree doesn't die— nor do we. Sometimes we wish we could. When God stabs that knife right to the heart and slices, sometimes we wish we could die. But the tears are what He collects, and it is the tears that bring the beautiful aroma of the spirit to everyone else.

Like the doubting Apostle Thomas, some people have to see the scars before they can believe. Sometimes we must share our scars, even our ravaged hearts, before they are convinced.

It's a hard lesson to learn, but we are a spiritual gift of frankincense as well as the gift of gold. It is our tears that bring forth this gift that was given on Christmas Day, the gift of frankincense.

I can remember once having asked God, "What am I going to do now with this frankincense, these tears, this rip in my heart, that you've allowed in my life?" Shortly afterward, I moved to Payson, Arizona, and I had no idea what I was going to do. I was tired of leading groups and of all the counseling and group activities I had been involved in. I was simply worn out. Knowing that the experiences I had gone through as a child were to come forth as gold, I realized they were to be shared at some time, but I didn't know how.

I had done twelve television programs for cable network in Phoenix. I had finished the series. It was all on tape and the tapes were my property. Someone suggested that I call the 700 Club to see if they would run them as a series. I contacted them and said, "I have a taped series, and I would like to play it on your station. Can you give me instruction as to how to proceed with this?"

Well, the lady I conversed with informed me that the only programs they used were paid for by the person submitting them and that it would cost me thousands of dollars to air my programs. She asked what the series was about, and I told her: *Total Brokenness*. It concerns all the difficulties that one experiences, how to overcome them and still be enthusiastic about life." She asked me to give her an example, and I thought, *she hasn't lived very long or hasn't experienced much hardship!*

Anyway, I shared with her a portion of my background. She remarked that Pat Roberts was doing a special program on overcoming the trauma of incest. She suggested that I come to Virginia to do a live broadcast for the 700 Club concerning my experiences in this regard. I thought to myself, *Oh, I don't think so!* I hadn't even told my children about my background at that particular time and had no intentions of doing so.

Then the Holy Spirit said, "Okay. This is what you've been prepared for." I thought, oh shoot! How do I do this? But I accepted, and I was sent a ticket to Virginia Beach. I was a bit frightened, because I had never done national television before, but it was an opening for me to do something to liberate others, to become the light that I was meant to be.

I remember sitting down with my children for a few hours and talking about it. They knew nothing about my past, and since the program was going to be on national television, I didn't want them to learn about it in school. Disclosing my history to them was my hardest and most emotional task.

When I boarded the plane, I had only one dollar in my pocket! I said, "God, I really need you to watch over me." A hotel had been provided for me and all the food that I could eat, and I ate lots! It had been arranged for me to be picked up by a limousine in Virginia Beach—this girl with a dollar in her pocket! Well, I arrived at the studio and did the program. They interviewed me for about half an hour. After it was over, I came back to the hotel emotionally drained.

I knew the Holy Spirit wasn't finished with me. I had carried one tape with me, which was titled "God's Timing." The theme was about moving in the right timing of God. When I entered the hotel lobby, the Spirit told me that this tape on God's timing was to be given to Pat Roberts. I thought, *Get serious!* He was running for President then, and the thought of approaching him scared me to death!

Nevertheless, I went into the dining room and sat down. I thought, *I don't know how I'm going to do this.* Lo and behold, Pat Roberts and five of his security men walked in. He sat down for lunch at the table right next to mine! My heart was going a hundred miles a minute! I thought, *Oh God! I can't believe that you really want me to do this!* I was terrified that Pat Roberts was going to think me terribly arrogant if I approached him, and I wondered how was I to get near him when he was surrounded by all those security men.

As if they had all gotten the signal at the same time to go to the men's room, they suddenly all walked out and left Mr. Roberts sitting there alone at the table. So I went over to him and said, "Excuse me, Sir, I'm so sorry to disturb you, and I don't mean to be intrusive, but I feel the Holy Spirit wants me to give you this." I handed him the tape of my program called "God's Timing."

He was most polite and gentle, and he said, "Thank you very much, I really appreciate this." He looked down at the title, then looked up and said, "I need this right now."

Four days later, Pat Roberts stopped running for President! I have no idea if my tape had anything to do with it, but I felt that I had really laid myself on the line by giving it to him. It all seemed unreal! But that's frankincense. If you will take the hurts in your life, the times you've been ripped to the heart, and use them to help others, it's your gift. There is no way of telling what situation the Spirit will place you in or in what way He will use you.

Myrrh

Last but not least is my favorite gift: myrrh. It is also extracted from a tree, a little myrrh tree. It's more like a bush, actually. It grows in Israel in sandy, stony places. It doesn't grow where there's nice fertile soil but where conditions are very, very difficult. It's a miracle plant. Small, not particularly pretty, producing only a few flowers, it grows in the hot, dry desert with very little water.

Many of you can relate to this plant spiritually. Perhaps you are in a similar situation in your spiritual lives now. We all have spiritual times that are terrific for us, and periods when we experience very dry times, yet we still need to produce. That's what the myrrh tree does.

My daughter has been going through this hot, dry place. She's been feeling much like a little tree that sits all alone and has a dry time. One weekend, Vanessa took her baby and went down to Phoenix to shop for Christmas. She had nearly $600 dollars, which she had saved. By evening she had spent around $60. Then she lost her wallet with all the money in it! After calling the police station in Chandler, she sat down and wept, because she'd been enduring so many hardships.

On Monday, she started back up the mountain to Payson. When a little over half way home, she hit black ice, spun three times into the mountain, and totaled her car! Although she and the baby walked away from the crash unscathed, she was probably wondering where God was in her life right then.

Yet out of every painful situation God will produce something wonderful, if you watch for it. When the myrrh branch is broken, a wonderful perfume is released! Because the tree perseveres through the hard and dry times this incredible incense is produced.

On the following Monday, Vanessa and I tried to figure out how she was going to pay her bills, since she had lost all her money. On top the pile of bills we discovered a letter from the Chandler Police Department. "Dear Ms. Fosholt: Your purse has been handed in to the Chandler Police Department with $529.60 in it." A little myrrh!

In every difficult situation, God hides a little miracle for you, if you will just have faith in Him. In you, he refines His gold, His frankincense, His myrrh, and produces, in you, His pearl of wisdom. No matter how unworthy you feel at times, you are becoming those gifts to the Christ.

Whether you consider the Christmas story an allegory or pure fact, it doesn't matter. What matters is that you have your own beliefs and allow others to have theirs.

Some tell us that Jesus wasn't born on December 25th, that He was born on such and such a day. I always thought to myself, if it were my birthday and everybody across the world was celebrating on the wrong day, would I care? Goodness no! I'd be excited that they loved me that much!

Many say that Christmas has become too commercial; but in spite of the cynicism in the world, I see an abundance of love. When folks give a dollar to the Salvation Army, or whatever charitable act they do, regardless of the reason, there is love in the air, and the message of love has been left for us. We just have to say, so what if it's gotten commercial, I'll do what I need to do to contribute. Let the love flow from *my* heart.

So think about the gifts the wise men brought to the Christ Child. Become those gifts, and present them to God in return for His gifts to you.

The End

ABOUT THE AUTHOR

Born in England, Vanda Millien became self-employed in the United States more than 25 years ago. During this time, she traveled extensively throughout America, connecting with its people, their spirit, humanity and challenges.

With a lively intelligence, quick wit, and personable manner, Vanda established a support group which grew from 12 persons to more than a hundred in a short period of time. As word spread about her effectiveness as a counselor, consultant, and speaker, she became much in demand by diverse groups and institutions requesting her for presentations, training programs, and inspirational talks.

Among Vanda's strengths is the ability to readily connect with the needs of her audience: speaking to businessmen in the forthright manner with which they are accustomed, conversing with young minds with all the playfulness and life of youth, counseling with such loving encouragement and gentle understanding so as to remove all barriers, and guiding a congregation on a journey of joy and heartfelt inspiration.

She has spoken before hundreds of groups during the last 15 years, hosted a weekly talk show for two years on Dimension Cable in Phoenix, Arizona, and was ordained a nondenominational minister in 1986. Vanda is equally at home in corporate boardrooms or leading organizational training sessons as she is in religious or philanthropic club settings, tackling the "real" problems of professional life and offering practical and meaningful solutions to them.

Her camera presence is as warm and lively as her personal appearances and is augmented by her relaxed, open qualities of honesty, insight, and caring. Her presentations are dynamic, informative, and empowering, fun-filled and effective. Her motivational presentations allow many to tap into their own inner resources, thus increasing their own personal effectiveness exponentially. Her overall goal is to stimulate each person to be happier, more productive, responsible and aware, and to make their personal "life's circumstances" work for rather than against them.

Words cannot adequately capture her unique, invisible qualities of knowingness and love.